Speaking Worlds:

Oral Histories from Bronx Regional High School

Speaking Worlds:
Oral Histories from Bronx Regional High School

Copyright © 2010
Student Press Initiative/Individual Authors

Founding Director, SPI: Erick Gordon
Alternative Education Coordinator, SPI: Jondou Chen
Speaking Worlds Coordinator, SPI: Courtney Brown

ISBN: 1-932948-86-4   978-1-932948-86-8

Collaborating New York City Department of Education Educators: Jackie Rangel, Yanira Rodriguez

SPI Educators: Katherine Arcos, Wilson Benito, Whitney Wood

Production Coordinator: Tiffany N. Aguilar
Project Administrator: Katie Campbell
Interior Layout and Design: Joseph Caffentzis
Assistant Editors: Rachel Kliegman, Guillermo Marini
Cover Design: Liz Starin
Photographs: Jondou J. Chen, Whitney Wood

Student Press Initiative
Teachers College, Columbia University
Box 182
525 West 120th Street
New York, NY 10027
www.publishspi.org

Acknowledgements

This publication would not have been possible were it not for our partnership with the GED Plus program of District 79 in the New York City Department of Education. Foremost, Robert Zweig, GED Plus Principal, and Assistant Principals Janet Declet and Barbara Diliberti were instrumental in partnering with SPI staff in creating the vision for the Speaking Worlds project. Furthermore, we appreciate GED Plus Assistant Principals Michelle Guzman, Collete Marshall, Dannete Miller, and Marie Polinsky for trusting the SPI process and encouraging and supporting our work with their students. Our staff members were also assisted at each GED Plus site by numerous Department of Education guidance counselors and paraprofessionals and New York City Police Department school safety officers.

In addition, accolades also go to a number of individuals who transcribed and translated the student work: Deluwara (Dinu) Ahmed (Bangla), Katherine Arcos (Spanish), Jeff Barnes (Creole), Wilson Benito (Spanish), James Chen (English), Paifei Chen (Mandarin), Alema (Shopna) Chowdhury (Bangla), Marc Cianciulli (Creole), Carmen Cianciulli (Creole), Hind Eideh (Arabic), Bertrand Fils-Aime (Creole), Kendra Hoerst (French), Michel Ligonde (French), Kinta Montilus (Creole), Victoria Norelid (Spanish) Shuchi Vyas (Gujarati). These individuals spent hours out of their own hectic schedules to provide accurate translations that stayed true to the student writer's voices. Finally, we wish to acknowledge the strength and the courage of each of our student authors who committed themselves to the Speaking Worlds project and can now be recognized as published authors.

Table of Contents

Journeys Past: Futures Forged
Nick Sousanis. 7

Foreword
Katherine Arcos, Wilson Benito
& Whitney Wood. 15

Prologue
Yanira A. Rodriguez 17

Prólogo
Yanira A. Rodriguez 17

Appreciations
Janet Declet. 19

Reflections: A Brief Note on Process
Courtney Brown, Jondou Chen
& Erick Gordon. 21

Rap Dreams
Blenfre Almonte. 25

He Who Follows Advice Reaches
Old Age
Angel Luis Aracena. 29

El Que Se Lleva Del Consejo
Llega a Viejo
Angel Luis Aracena. 31

El Artista-B2
Yan Carlos Bido 35

El Artista B2
Yan Carlos Bido 36

I Miss My Country
El Mejor. 39

Extraño a Mi País
El Novio. 40

How Would You Feel in Jail?
Sindy 43

¿Cómo Te Sentirías al Estar en
Una Cárcel?
Sindy 44

My Dedication to Studying
Henry Cepin. 49

Mi Dedicación en los Estudios
Henry Cepin. 51

My Father is the Most Wonderful
Person in My Life
Natasha De La Cruz. 55

Mi Papá es Lo Más Maravilloso en
Mi Vida
Niza De La Cruz 57

The New Revolution
Arafat La Leyenda. 61

La Nueva Revolución
Arafat La Leyenda. 62

Fighting for a Dream
Adrian Gonzalez. 65

Luchando Por un Sueño
Adrian Gonzalez. 67

My Passion for Baseball
David 73

La Pasión Por el Baseball
David 74

The Child of God
Chiquito. 77

El Niño de Dios
Chiquito. 78

Everything I've Been Through
Jacquie 81

Todo Lo Que He Pasado
Jacquie 83

Life in Two Nations
Musa Jobarteh. 87

Love from Afar, Over the Distance
Veronica Lizardo 91

El Amor de Lejos, Entre la Distancia
Veronica Lizardo 93

Thanks to God
Francisco 97

Gracias a Dios
Francisco 98

My Life in the Dominican Republic and New York
Jose Gabriel Muñoz 101

Mi Vida en Republica Dominicana y New York
José Gabriel Muñoz 102

Life's Injustice
Trujillo 105

La Injusticia de la Vida
Trujillo 106

Don't Hold Back On Happiness
Anabel Peralta 111

No Se Limite en Darle Felicidad
Anabel Peralta 113

My Story and My Family's Story
Pimentel 117

Mi Historia y la de Mi Familia
Pimentel 119

Alejandro, the Blessing of My Life
Leticia 123

La Bendición De Mi Vida Es Alejandro
Leticia 125

Has Destiny Ever Changed Your Beliefs?
Lisael Ovalle 129

¿El Destino Alguna Vez Le Ha Cambiado Sus Ilusiones?
Lisael Ovalle 131

My World Changed Thanks to You
La Negra Rodriguez 135

Mi Mundo Cambio Gracias A Tí
La Negra Rodriguez 137

The Path of Hope
Yomari Salcedo 141

El Camino de la Esperanza
Yomari Salcedo 142

Separation Causes a Family Harm
Cesar 145

La Separación Ocasiona Daños En La Familia
Cesar 146

How Would You Feel?
Santos Memories 149

¿Cómo Te Sentirías Perder a Alguien Tan Especial en Tu Vida?
Santos Memories 151

Soccer is Just Like a War, but Sometimes Much More Than a War
Moussa Sinerna 155

My Heart
Ramon Noel Tavarez 159

Mi Corazón
Ramon Noel Tavarez 161

My Baby
Lilibeth Vargas 165

OUR STORIES START WITH OUR NAMES.

FOR SHADAD, CHILDHOOD WAS THE BEST TIME OF HIS LIFE.

BUT AS MANY DO, THEY HAVE TO GROW UP FAST. THE GIRL WITH AN ABSENT FATHER IS TEASED RELENTLESSLY.

NAMED FOR A LOST OLDER BROTHER, AMIN ALO'S NAME ("TO BELIEVE"/"SUN") SHAPES HIS STORY.

FREE FROM RESPONSIBILITY, CHILDHOOD MEANT

INNOCENCE,

LOVE,

AND HOPE.

UNTIL ONE DAY HE RETURNS, SOOTHING HER HEART AND A PHOTO OF THEIR REUNION ENDS CRUEL TAUNTS. AND MARIE SAYS, "NOW I KNOW MY FATHER."

IN ORDER TO PROVIDE FOR THEIR CHILDREN TO GO TO SCHOOL, KATIE'S PARENTS LIVED APART FROM THEIR CHILDREN — IT WAS HARD BUT SHE UNDERSTOOD.

AND WHEN HER MOTHER FINALLY EARNED ENOUGH MONEY TO SEND HER TO SCHOOL WITH HER FRIENDS, TENZIN CRIED JOYFULLY.

THE THREAT OF VIOLENCE PREVENTED ANGELO FROM GOING TO SCHOOL — IT WAS TOO DANGEROUS: "I SAW SOME THINGS THAT A CHILD SHOULDN'T SEE."

SEDDIK SAW ONLY WAR AND OPPRESSION. ANY RESISTANCE WAS FORCEFULLY STAMPED OUT — A BOY THROWING A ROCK AT A TANK IS BLINDED IN A HAIL OF BULLETS.

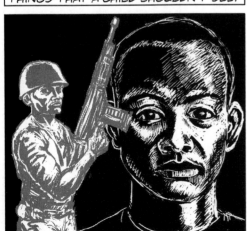

HIS PEOPLE BARRED FROM MOVING FREELY,

NOT ONLY COULDN'T HE GO TO SCHOOL, HE COULDN'T LEAVE HIS HOUSE AND NEVER WENT OUTSIDE.

PRISONERS IN THEIR OWN HOME.

A BOY SPEEDING ON A MOTORBIKE,

AND THEN A TERRIBLE BLAST.

AMIR SEES IT ALL, ENROUTE TO MEET HIS FRIENDS.

FRIENDS WHOM HE MUST NOW FIND AND IDENTIFY IN THE RUBBLE

AS HE HAS TO TELL THEIR DISBELIEVING MOTHERS THAT THEIR BOYS AREN'T COMING HOME AGAIN.

BUT HIS TORMENT DOESN'T STOP THERE,

SOME TRAGEDIES ARE NATURAL, BUT NO LESS PAINFUL.

THE EARTH QUAKES AND SPLITS, IN HER TERROR, JESSICA PRAYED AND PROMISES TO LIVE A BETTER LIFE.

AND AFTERWARDS, VANESSA OBSERVES:

"LIFE CAN CHANGE IN AN INSTANT - GOOD OR BAD"

EVEN IN THE MIDST OF EVERYTHING, LIFE GOES ON.

IN RESPONSE TO BEING TOLD WHO SHE CAN LOVE, SYEDA PROTESTS, "I'M NOT A FLOWER" AND DEFIANTLY ASSERTS HER RIGHT TO CHOOSE LOVE ALL HER OWN.

YES, THIS SEARCH SOMETIMES LEADS TO A BROKEN HEART, YET THEY PERSIST UNDAUNTED...

GERALDA LONGS FOR ONE WHO CAN READ THE SECRETS IN HER HEART.

A BOY WHO CAN EMBRACE HER TO SILENCE WITH HIS KISS.

WHILE LEARNING A NEW LANGUAGE IS DIFFICULT,

SO INTENT UPON TELLING THEIR STORIES, THEY OVERCOME ALL OBSTACLES.

AS SHADAD OBSERVES, "LOOKING AT THE PAST POINTS US TO THE FUTURE." THEY SEE THE POWER IN THEIR STORIES TO TEACH AND HELP OTHERS.

BUT THEY NEED TO HAVE A SPACE IN WHICH TO SHARE THEIR STORIES. THIS MEANS **TEACHING IS NOT**

FILLING STUDENTS UP WITH KNOWLEDGE,

IN A ONE-DIRECTIONAL FLOW FROM TEACHER TO STUDENT.

JOHN DEWEY DEFINED CAPACITY NOT AS AN EMPTINESS TO BE FILLED, BUT AS A "FORCE POSITIVELY PRESENT" — POTENTIAL TO BE DEVELOPED.

FOR SPI'S ERICK GORDON, STUDENTS ARE "CONTAINERS OF STORIES" WHO BRING THE BASIS FOR CURRICULUM WITH THEM INTO THE CLASSROOM.

IN ORDER TO CREATE THIS OPENING FOR POSSIBILITIES **TEACHING IS**

RECOGNIZING THAT STUDENTS COME WITH A WEALTH OF EXPERIENCES, AND LEARNING IS MULTI-DIRECTIONAL — IT TAKES PLACE ALONGSIDE ONE ANOTHER IN A COMMUNITY.

BY LEARNING TO LISTEN

WE COME TO SEE ALL THAT WE SHARE IN OUR STRUGGLES AND OUR JOY,

DISSOLVING WALLS (BOTH LITERAL AND METAPHORICAL) THAT STOOD BETWEEN US.

TAMARA IMAGINES PEOPLE READING HER STORY AND THINKING ABOUT THEIR OWN LIVES.

AND IN TURN THEY SHARE THEIR OWN STORIES AND INSPIRE NEW DREAMS...

THIS HAS BEEN
JOURNEYS PAST; FUTURES FORGED

A QUILT OF STORIES FASHIONED BY
NICK SOUSANIS

AS TOLD TO BY **SPI TEACHERS** AND **DISTRICT 79 AUTHORS**

WITH GRATITUDE AND RESPECT FOR ALL.

WWW.PUBLISHSPI.ORG

NSOUSANIS@GMAIL.COM
SPINWEAVEANDCUT.COM

FONTS BY COMICRAFT.COM

Foreword

Katherine Arcos, Wilson Benito & Whitney Wood
Student Press Initiative

Working with the students and faculty at Bronx Regional's GED Plus program proved to be a noticeably transformative experience. Each day we trudged from the elevated Prospect Avenue subway station lamenting our frozen fingers or marveling at the clear blue sky on our way to the high school. In contrast, as we retraced our steps after the two-hour class session each day, the weather garnered no airtime. Our enlivened conversation centered on the unstoppable support of the school staff and the tenacity and bravery of our students. We were inspired by their work ethic and openness in the writing process, the diversity of their dynamic stories, and the wisdom they shared in the retelling of their lives. We celebrated the way you could hear a pin drop as the students tackled prewriting activities or the enthusiasm with which they participated in group discussions. Each day, we left honored and humbled by the depth and intensity of the experiences our seemingly carefree students shared in their interviews and writing. The difference in our step and chatter before and after visiting the school parallels the change we experienced through the process of producing this book.

As teachers, we have been indelibly marked by the dedication and generosity we experienced at Bronx Regional. We are especially grateful to Ms. Rodriguez and Ms. Rangel whose ongoing assistance and hands-on involvement were instrumental. Each and every day, we counted on them to help students brainstorm ideas or refocus their attention and most importantly to motivate them during harder moments. We'd also like to thank Assistant Principals Michelle Guzman and Janet Declet, whose vision made our project possible.

Whether they took a plane or walked day and night without food, all of these authors made their own transformative journeys, not only in coming to New York, but also in telling their stories. In this volume you will find tales of receiving visas and missing home, memories of family and travel, and hopes of reuniting with loved ones left behind. We invite you to take your own journey as you page through the stories offered here. If you are touched by the strength, hard work, and sincerity of these student authors in any fraction of the degree to which we were over the past semester, the potential of this book has been achieved. Happy reading!

Prologue

Yanira A. Rodriguez
ESL Teacher, GED Plus at Bronx Regional

The following autobiographies will reveal the truth about my students. In the following pages you will get to know students from all over the world. Their constant effort, diligence and great interest to survive in a culture completely different from their country of origin greatly moved me.

The GED students I work with are students full of desire, peace and motivation. I am very proud of them and their work in the past couple of months, from the beginning of the writing program until the end.

I feel immensely honored and privileged to have participated in this exciting program with Columbia University and my students.

Prólogo

Yanira A. Rodriguez
ESL Teacher, GED Plus at Bronx Regional

Las siguientes autobiografías revelan las verdades de mis estudiantes. En las proximas páginas conocerán estudiantes de todas partes del mundo. Su constante esfuerzo, diligencia y gran interés por sobrevivir en una cultura muy diferente a su país natal me emocionarón.

Ellos son jovenes adultos llenos de fuerza, paz y motivación. Estoy muy orgullosa de ellos y de su trabajo en los ultimos meses, del principio al final del programa de escritura.

Me siento sumamente feliz y orgullosa de haber participado en este exitoso programa con Columbia University y mis estudiantes.

Appreciations

Janet Declet
Assistant Principal, GED Plus at Bronx Regional

I am extremely proud of the autobiographies our students have written. The writings focus on their life experience in their native country and in the United States. The effort and motivation that transpired in the classroom truly strengthened my belief that all of our students want to succeed and that each of them have a story to tell.

The Student Press Initiative helped our students tell their stories. I want to thank all the individuals involved in this wonderful project. I also want to thank Ms. Rodriguez, Ms. Rangel, and all the other GED professionals involved for their persistence and their commitment to this project and to our students.

It was an honor for me to read these wonderful stories and to have students share their experiences with me.

Reflections: A Brief Note on Process

Courtney Brown, Jondou Chen & Erick Gordon
Student Press Initiative

The voices in Speaking Worlds are as unique and individual as their authors. Yet, as a collection, these stories map the common territory of newly immigrated students between the ages of 17-21. The authors of these stories came to New York from over 15 countries and speak over 22 different languages. Each author is an emerging English speaker studying at a GED Plus school in New York City and forging a new life here. Each author has not only written his or her own story, but is authoring his or her new life as an adult in a new land.

These stories take us on journeys to childhood experiences around the globe, border-crossings, reunions and separations from loved ones, births and deaths, and suggestions of chapters not yet written. Speaking from many worlds, these stories have the power to touch us all.

The stories in these books are the culmination of months of collaboration between ESL teachers at five alternative education sites around New York City and our SPI educators who led the students through a process of discovering and recording their oral histories, and then crafting their stories into chapters for publication.

The students engaged in multiple phases of the project: from studying the discipline of oral history, to intimate interviews, transcription, and finally drafting and revising their pieces for publication. It was a rigorous process, and one through which, at times, it was difficult to envision an end. The use of voice recording technology allowed the students to be interviewed in their native languages, as needed, in order to access the depth and maturity of their voices and stories. This process was highly individual—stories were told, only to be deleted, and stories untold were discovered and written later into a draft. Once an interview was completed, its transcription became a working draft that the students proceeded to "craft" into their final stories—intently focusing on revising the overall piece and fine-tuning the details of sentence structure, grammar and punctuation. Throughout the process, the students built their English literacy skills, shared, conferred and bonded across and within cultural lines. The classrooms hummed at times with creative energy, and at other times, vibrated with silent intensity, as students worked to perfect their stories.

As with any new project, we learned as we went. As the project progressed, and we strove to fulfill the needs of each site and its students, our team expanded. We reached out to native speakers, colleagues, friends and family members, who spoke the languages of our students—Bangla, Creole, Arabic, Spanish, Urdu, Mandarin, Hindi, French, and others; all of whom helped interview and support the students, on site, as well as translating and transcribing, off site.

This project could not have happened without the team of remarkable, dedicated individuals who contributed to it. The list of those we'd like to thank reaches from Bogota, Columbia, where Victoria Norelid translated and edited Spanish drafts, to the Palestinian territories, where Hind Eideh worked in Arabic, to Jeff Barnes working in Creole in Cambridge, Massachusetts, and James and Paifei Chen working in Mandarin in Los Angeles, California.

Starting here in New York, we'd like to thank Assistant Principals Barbara Diliberti and Janet Declet for having the vision and faith to partner with SPI to pilot this project, and for continuing to support us on-site. We'd also like to thank the wonderful site leaders who supported us at Bronx Regional, the Jamaica Learning Center, the Linden Learning Center, and the Alternative Education Complex: Assistant Principals Michelle Guzman, Collette Hendricks, Dannete Miller and Marie Polinsky.

Thank you to our incredible collaborating teachers at each site: Mr. Pedro DeLlano and Ms. Jessica Slote at Tenzer Center, Ms. Rosalie Reeves and Mr. Robert Kauffman at Jamaica Learning Center, Ms. Jill Yablon and Ms. Jessica White at the Alternative Education Center, Ms. Jackie Rangel and Ms. Yanira Rodriguez at Bronx Regional, and Dr. Bradley Jordan, Mr. Joe Avella and Mr. Pierre Balthazar at Linden Learning Center. Thank you for talking the students through their issues and keeping them on track —telling one's story is not always easy!

Thank you to our twelve absolutely fantastic site instructors for taking the journey with us and trusting that its snags and twisting turns would eventually get us to the place we are now. Your flexibility, fortitude, patience and humanity have gotten us here. Dinu Ahmed, Ruth Aman, Katherine Arcos, Wilson Benito, Julia Benjamin, Suzanne Choo, Kendra Hoerst, Erin Lynch, Marcelle Mentor, Brice Particelli, Denise Mensah-Daniels, and Whitney Wood, we are so grateful for all that you did.

Behind many projects there are less visible heroes. We'd like to acknowledge our terrific "behind the scenes" team: Tiffany Aguilar jumped into the project to take on the role of art director, Christina Shon, aided by Katie Campbell, took on the extra office work required; Hailey Kim added new design work to her schedule. Erin and Whitney "wore extra hats", Kerry McKibbin, offered her wisdom about the phases of the project and Rachel Kliegman helped with final edits! Evan Smith-Rakoff, your design work is superb. To Eynat Amir, Eric Haak, Althea Jack, Kinta Montilus, and Anne Winiarksi thank you all for acknowledging the students' hard work and writing them letters of feedback.

To our fabulous visiting artists—Nick Sousanis, Laura Starcheski and Kate Rosenbloom—thank you so much for documenting the project and adding to it yet another layer of beauty and complexity. It is our hope that through the stories Nick captures in comic form, Laura in audio and Kate in video, our readers, viewers and listeners will feel a little closer to the remarkable students we were fortunate enough to work with in these classrooms.

Most of all, students, we are struck with profound gratitude. Thank you for sharing your lives with us. We believe in you, in the power of your stories and in your strength and resilience.

Gracias, Dhanyavad, Merci, Shukran, Mese, Tujechhe, Xie Xie…Thank you.

Rap Dreams

Blenfre Almonte
Dominican Republic

My name is Blenfre Almonte. I was born here, but after nine months my mother and I went to the Dominican Republic, because we didn't like it here. I lived in the Dominican Republic all my life until seven months ago. Then, I came to New York, and I am studying here. This is my last year in the GED program.

I live here with my father, but the rest of my family is in the Dominican Republic. I have come back because I am looking for the best life here, because there is opportunity in New York. Opportunity like schools, universities, colleges, and GED programs, like this one. Like here I am writing something about my life! In the Dominican Republic they don't have these programs, because they are poor, you know? But it is my country. I feel good about writing something about my life. Now this is my opportunity, right?

My dream is to be a rapper. This has been my dream since I was born. I write songs, because it is my passion. I want to be like Lil Wayne, because he is my favorite artist. I have visited a music studio and tried the microphone, but I haven't recorded because I am not ready yet. I just write the rap now, the lyrics, for the moment.

I think that I came out like my mother, because she wanted to sing when she was a young girl. She imitated Ana Gabriel in a singing competition for romantic music. She won some awards. She was 18 years old at this time, in 1982. My mother and I have the same desire, but with different kinds of music. All of my family likes music. When I am writing new music I call my mother, "Mom, you hear? Can you hear? Let me show you my new music," and she listens and says, "Fantastic!" You know how mothers are. When something is bad or sad for me, she always says, "You can, you can!"

It is important to me to get my GED because then I can go to college. I want to study fixing computers or carpentry because those are good jobs. I can keep writing music all the time, but I can finish college quickly, and then I can write my music and play my music on the radio, CD, you know… My mother and my grandmother want this for me.

With my music, I want to tell people about work, about relationships, about the world, about my life, my family, and all of this. It is important to tell people about all of this so they can learn more about me, about the world, about life on the street, about all of this. My message is to not use drugs; don't fight with your family. Don't do that. Don't fight with the police. And then you can follow all the dreams that you have in your mind.

This is the life for me—the music. I was born with this dream in my mind. I think that pursuing your dreams will lead to success in life.

He Who Follows Advice Reaches Old Age

Angel Luis Aracena
Dominican Republic

Advice is very important in life. In my case, advice has been very valuable. I was very excited when I was coming to New York, but an aunt of mine died shortly before my flight. Nine days after her death, my uncle died. Since I can't talk about how they died, I will talk about their lives.

My aunt played, but we always argued. I used to fight with my aunt Rosmeris, but I always ate what she left in the kitchen. Despite the fights with my aunt, I loved her. One day, I asked her for ten dollars, and she told me she didn't have any money. She called me and said, "You think I'm your mother?" And then she gave it to me. I always washed my uncle Elvis' car and ran every errand that he asked me to. He gave me money, and I didn't have to ask for it. My uncle always made fun of me and he would pinch my hair. He also used to give me tickets for the national lottery. I was very sad when they died, because I always used to see my aunt sitting near the door of my house and my uncle always passed by my house and gave me tickets. I also miss my great-grandmother, who gave me a lot of advice.

When I left my country, I also had to leave my grandmother, the person who raised me. I love her a lot. She fought with me a lot because I was a brat, and I didn't listen to what she would tell me. When she told me something, I would tell her to leave me alone.

My family has always helped me, especially my grandmother, my aunt Rosmeris, and my uncle Elvis. They gave me advice, even though I was a brat. My grandmother would tell me, "You are not going outside," but I went anyway and returned at dawn. She wouldn't sleep until I came back.

I also remember the advice that my neighbors would give me. Braulio told me to study and to not follow anyone. My other neighbor Angelina told me to ask instead of steal. She would tell me that if life gave me something, it's all right, and if it didn't give me anything, it is also all right. I was hungry one day and I told her, "I am hungry."

"Just like that, instead of robbing, it is better to ask," she responded. I felt good, because one day I went to a river and I was hungry. There was a lady who was making soup and I asked for some. She gave it to me. I remembered the advice that my neighbor had given me. My friend Edward told me to behave and to study so that I wouldn't go through any hardship, and so that I'd have things when I got older. He also told me that drugs are trash that destroys people. Those who use them can never become someone; they will only become trash in the middle of the road.

When I recall my childhood, I think about my family members and my friends. I also remember a time of difficulty. I was working and a door fell on my hand. I came home and my aunt asked me why my hand was swollen. When I fell asleep, a huge pain started in my hand, and my grandmother took me to the hospital. I had to stay in the hospital, because I had an infection and they had to operate on my hand. The doctor told me that I could possibly lose my hand. I found a syringe and poked the part of my hand that was swollen because they couldn't operate if it stayed that way. The next morning, the doctor saw my hand and squeezed it and said it was fine. They discharged me from the hospital and I went home.

I learned a lot from this experience, because I realized how much my grandmother really cared for me. The same way that I was crying, she would cry, and she couldn't stand to see me in that predicament. I also learned that even though you can be a brat, no matter how bad you are, your mother or grandmother will always love you. I felt good because my grandmother told me that you only get one life and you have to appreciate it.

Now, I am in New York studying to prepare myself to go to college and choose my profession. I want to work so that I can have a house in Santo Domingo and a business to help support me. I have learned that not everything lasts forever. If someday your mother or someone older gives you advice, take it. Don't get mad, and never play deaf, because you don't know if you'll need that advice tomorrow.

El Que Se Lleva Del Consejo Llega a Viejo

Angel Luis Aracena
Dominican Republic

Los consejos son muy importantes en esta vida. En mi caso, los consejos han sido muy valiosos. Yo estaba muy alegre cuando venía para Nueva York pero hubo una tía mía que murió poco antes de me viaje. A los 9 días de su muerte, murió otro tío mío. Esto me dolió mucho. Ya que no puedo hablar sobre como murieron, voy hablar sobre como fueron sus vidas.

Mi tía jugaba conmigo, pero siempre discutíamos. Peleaba mucho con mi tía Rosmeris, pero siempre comía lo que dejaba en la cocina. A pesar de los pleitos de mi tía, yo la quería. Un día le pedí a mi tía que me diera diez pesos y ella me dijo que no tenía. Me llamo y me dijo, "¿Tu crees que yo soy tu mamá?" Y después me los dio. A mi tío Elvis siempre le lavaba el carro y iba a todos los mandados que el me pedía. Me daba dinero sin pedirle. Mi tío siempre me relajaba y me daba pellizcos. También me daba billetes de la lotería nacional. Yo estaba muy triste cuando murieron porque siempre veía a mi tía en la puerta de mi casa sentada y mi tío siempre pasaba por mi casa y me daba billetes. También extraño a mi bisabuela, que me daba muchos consejos.

Cuando me fui de mi país, también tuve que dejar a mi abuela, que fue quien me crió. La quiero mucho. Peleaba mucho conmigo porque yo era malcriado con ella y no le hacía caso a lo que me decía. Cuando ella me decía algo, yo le decía que no me joda.

Mi familia siempre me ayudó, especialmente mi abuela, mi tía Rosmeris, y mi tío Elvis. Me daban consejos aunque yo era malcriado. Mi abuela me decía, "No vas a salir," pero yo me iba como quiera y llegaba de madrugada. Hasta que no llegaba ella no se dormía.

También me acuerdo de lo consejos que mis vecinos me daban. Braulio me dijo que estudiara y que no me llevara de nadie. Mi otra vecina Angelina me decía que en vez de robar, que pidiera. Ella me decía que si la vida me daba, estaba bien, y si no me daba, también estaba bien. Un día yo tenía hambre y yo le dije a ella misma, "Yo tengo hambre." "Así mismo hazlo, en vez de robar, mejor pide," me contesto. Me sentí bien porque un día fui a un rió y yo tenia hambre. Había una mujer que estaba haciendo un ensopado y yo le pedí. Y ella me lo dio. Me acordé del consejo que me dio mi vecina. Mi amigo Edward me dijo que me portara bien y que estudiara para que no pasara trabajo y para que tenga algo cuando sea grande. Me dijo también que las drogas son una basura que destruyen las personas. Quien usa eso no vuelve a ser más gente si no una basura en el medio del camino.

Cuando recuerdo mi infancia, pienso en mis familiares y mis amistades. También me acuerdo de un momento muy difícil. Yo estaba trabajando y me cayó una puerta en la mano. Llegué a casa y mi tía me preguntó porque tenía la mano hinchada. Cuando me acosté, comenzó un dolor fuerte en la mano y mi abuela me llevó al hospital. Me dejaron internado porque tenía una infección y me tenían que operar. El doctor me dijo que posiblemente podía perder mi mano. Busque una jeringa y me ponché la parte que estaba hinchada, porque no la podían operar si seguía así. La mañana siguiente el doctor me vio la mano y me la apretó y dijo que estaba bien. Me dieron de alta y me fui para casa.

Aprendí mucho de este momento porque sentí que mi abuela me quería de verdad. Así mismo que yo lloraba, ella lloraba también y no podía aguantar verme así en esa situación. También aprendí que aunque uno sea malcriado—por más malo que uno sea—su madre o abuela siempre lo van a querer. Me sentí bien porque mi abuela me dijo a mí que la vida es solo una y hay que valorarla.

Ahora estoy en Nueva York estudiando para prepararme para ir a la universidad y elejir mi profesión. Quiero trabajar para tener una casa en Santo Domingo y un negocio para poder mantenerme. Aprendí que no todo dura para siempre. Si algun día tu madre o alguien mayor te da un consejo, cógelo. No te enojes ni nunca te hagas el sordo porque no sabes si en el mañana necesites ese consejo.

El Artista-B2

Yan Carlos Bido
Dominican Republic

I am B2. They call me that because my name is quite long. I discovered my talent when I was four years old. When I was little, I didn't draw as well, we could say. But with time, I got better and better. I am very thoughtful and always keep busy with drawing, practicing Tae Kwon Do, and writing mambo songs. I am very dedicated and friendly but with a serious face. I am a bit quiet, but I like to listen.

Whenever I'm bored, I draw. I can draw anything I see, as I see it, but I especially like drawing caricatures. I make drawings that are messages—drawings that have meaning and things that I imagine. Sometimes I make drawings that many people don't understand. But they can understand by simply concentrating and paying attention to the drawing, and thus understanding its message. The drawing that I speak of is something religious. In the picture there was a man who was in hell. He extended his hand to God and said, "My God, please don't abandon me." The man felt abandoned, alone, sad, and needed God's help. God extended his hand to him. At that time, I was going through many things. Everything was going wrong, and I felt sad and abandoned. That's why I decided to draw my feelings and the image was about my life.

If I could draw a story, it would be of action and adventure, but those themes include a bit of violence. I would have to think of something that isn't too violent because I would like to include something positive, not negative. Action and adventure movies have a lot of things with bad people, like guns, criminals and murderers, and it is important for me to include something positive because it would be much better for children who read my story to not grow up with such a negative mindset. I would also love to illustrate a book that is interesting to adults, but also has a good message.

I came here with my mother and my two brothers. My sister and my dad stayed behind. They have to wait in order to come to the United States. I hope they come soon.

I would like to live here, because there are more opportunities for those who study. I came here when I was only thirteen years old, and I enrolled in a school. At that time, English was difficult for me. I didn't understand anything when teachers spoke to me in English, and it was complicated for me to understand what was going on and what we were studying. But with time I adapted and that's how I learned. So now I can speak English, but I need to practice more. Every time people ask me something, I respond in English. I'm in a GED program because I want to get an MBA and become a professional artist like a graphic designer or illustrator.

El Artista B2

Yan Carlos Bido
Dominican Republic

Yo soy B2. Me llaman así porque mi nombre es bastante largo. Descubrí mi talento cuando tenía cuatro años. Cuando yo era pequeño no dibujaba tan bien que digamos. Pero a través del tiempo, lo hacía mejor y mejor. Yo soy muy pensativo y siempre me mantengo ocupado. Me fascina dibujar, practicar Tae Kwon Do y escribir canciones de mambo. Soy un joven muy decidido y amable pero con cara seria, un poco callado pero me gusta escuchar.

Cuando estoy aburrido, me pongo a dibujar. Puedo dibujar cualquier cosa que yo vea, tal como se ve, pero me gusta dibujar caricaturas en especial. Hago dibujos que son mensajes—dibujos que tienen significado y cosas que me imagino. A veces hago dibujos que muchas personas no entienden. Pero lo pueden entender simplemente concentrándose y poniéndole atención al dibujo y así comprenderán cual es el mensaje que tiene. El dibujo del cual hablo es algo religioso. En el cuadro, había un hombre que estaba en el infiero. Le tendía su mano a Dios y decía, "Dios mío, por favor no me abandones." Dios estaba dándole la mano. El hombre se sentía abandonado, solo, y triste y necesitaba la ayuda de Dios. En ese tiempo me estaban pasando muchas cosas malas. Todo me estaba yendo mal y me sentí triste y abandonado. Por eso decidí dibujar mis sentimientos y la imagen era yo.

Si pudiera dibujar una historia, sería de acción y aventura, pero en esos temas se incluye un poco de violencia. Tendría que pensar en algo que no sea tan violento porque me gustaría incluir algo que tenga algo positivo no algo negativo. Las películas de acción y aventura tienen muchas cosas de gente mala como pistolas, criminales y asesinatos, y es importante para mi incluir algo positivo porque seria mucho mejor que los niños que lo lean no crezcan con una mente negativa. Me gustaría ilustrar un libro que sea interesante para adultos pero que también tenga un mensaje bueno.

Vine aquí con mi madre y mis dos hermanos. Se quedó mi hermana y mi padre. Tiene que esperar para poder venir a los Estados Unidos. Yo espero que muy pronto vengan.

Me gusta vivir aquí porque hay más oportunidades para aquellos quienes estudian. Vine aquí cuando tenía solamente trece años y me inscribí en una escuela. En ese entonces, se me hacía difícil el inglés. No entendía absolutamente nada cuando los maestros hablaban en inglés y se me era complicado entender lo que estaba pasando y sobre que estaban estudiando. Pero con el tiempo me adapté y así fue que aprendí. So now I can speak English, but I need to practice more. Every time people ask me something I respond in English. I'm in a GED program because I want to get an MBA and become a professional artist like a graphic designer or illustrator.

I Miss My Country

El Mejor
Ecuador

I am a kid who likes to enjoy life. I arrived in New York on February 4th, 2009, on a very cold night. It was the saddest day of my life when I came to live in the United States, after leaving the people I knew—my friends and my girlfriends. My first few days here, I felt very weird. I wasn't in a familiar environment. I didn't feel the same; I felt suffocated, like the life had been sucked out of me. I didn't know anyone, and I felt very alone. I don't like this country because of the people, the city, and the lifestyle. I don't like the Bronx. It's ugly with really old buildings, and I was expecting to see more Americans and not as many Latinos.

When I got here, I went to live with my mom, my brothers, and my stepfather. I came with my sister, and later, my other sisters came too, and now we're all here together. My mom moved to New York when I was still very little, only two years old. After ten years, she returned to Ecuador, when I was about thirteen, and it was very strange to see her again. Now that I'm living with her for the first time, I'm not happy, because I don't like living with my mom. She doesn't let me go out, and I don't have any freedom to be able to go dancing, go out with my friends, go to the movies, skating, and have fun. My life here is nothing compared to my past life. I go to school and back home. I study, do my homework, and eat. At five pm, I go pick up my sister from school, and then we eat dinner. Then the routine is repeated the next day. And that's how I've spent the past year and two months in this country. I wanted to go back to

Ecuador when my grandmother passed away, but the tickets were too expensive, and my mom didn't let me go. I was so sad.

In Ecuador, I had a great life, worry free. I had school friends and neighborhood friends. My friends and I always went to parties, played soccer or volleyball; we were always together for everything. I also miss my girlfriend, who is very beautiful. Before moving here, my friends threw me a going-away party. It was the best party that I've ever had. The day before moving here was the best day of my life, because I was with all my friends.

But, I've had one good experience in this country. Two months ago, I visited Chicago, and, for the first time, I felt great. I would really like to live in Chicago, because it's really pretty. I don't know why, but I just liked it a lot more than I like New York. I have two girlfriends in Ecuador, two in Chicago, and I also have friends in Chicago. They understand me. It's not the same living with my mom. With my friends, I can talk about everything—sad things, happy things, difficult things… everything, everything. One day, I'd like to move to Chicago or return to Ecuador.

Extraño a Mi País

El Mejor
Ecuador

Yo soy un chico que le gusta disfrutar de la vida. Yo llegué a New York el 4 de febrero del 2009, una noche muy helada. Fue el día más triste de mi vida cuando vine acá a los Estados Unidos y dejé a todos mis familiares, mis amigos, y mis novias. Mis primeros días aquí me sentía extraño. No me sentía en el mismo ambiente que en mi país. Me sentía como que no era lo mismo, como ya muy encerrado, como que si ya no tenía vida. No conocía a nadie y me sentía solo. No me gusta este país por la gente, la ciudad, y el estilo de vida. No me gustaba el Bronx. Era muy feo con los edificios muy viejos yo pensaba ver mas gringos que latinos.

Cuando llegué aquí vivía en el Bronx con mi mamá, mis hermanos y mi padrastro. Yo vine con mi hermana primero y luego vinieron mis otras hermanas y estamos todos juntos ahí. Mi mamá vino a vivir aquí cuando era pequeñito todavía, 2 años. A los 10 años volvió a Ecuador, cuando yo ya tenía como 13 y me sentía raro al verla. Ahora que tengo que vivir con ella por primera vez, no estoy contento porque no me gusta mucho vivir con mi mamá. No me deja salir y me falta mucha libertad como ir a bailar, salir con mis amigos, ir al cine, patinar, todo eso. Mi vida aquí no se compara a mi pasado. Voy a mi casa, de ahí para la escuela. Estudio, como, hago mi tarea. A las 5 voy a recoger a mi hermana a la escuela y después cenamos. Luego repito todo el próximo día. Y así pasé un año y dos meses que estoy en este país. Quería regresar antes a Ecuador porque falleció mi abuela y como los pasajes estaban muy caros no me dejó ir. Me sentía muy triste.

En Ecuador, yo la pasaba bien de todo, sin problemas ni nada. Allá tengo amigos de la escuela y del barrio. Siempre con mis amigos iba a fiestas, a jugar soccer o vóley y siempre estábamos juntos para todo. También tenía a mi novia que es muy hermosa. Antes de venir acá, mis amigos me hicieron una fiesta de despedida. Fue el mejor party que tuve y estuvo muy bonito. El último día antes de venir acá fue el día más bonito porque pude estar con todos mis amigos reunidos.

Pero también he tenido una experiencia buena en este país. Hace dos meses, cuando visité la ciudad de Chicago por primera vez me sentía super. Me gustaría mucho vivir en Chicago porque es bien bonito. No sé, me gustó más que New York. Yo tengo dos novias en Ecuador y dos en Chicago, y también tengo amigos que viven en Chicago. Ellos me entienden en todo. No es lo mismo que estar con mi mamá. Con ellos hablo de todas las cosas que pasan—cosas tristes, alegres, lo más difícil… Todo, todo. Algún día me gustaría mudarme a Chicago o volver al Ecuador.

How Would You Feel in Jail?

Sindy
Mexico

When I decided to move to the US from Mexico, I drove across the border with a fake visa. I got really nervous and scared when immigration asked me for my visa. They told me to get out of the car and started asking me questions. When they took me to their office, they realized that the visa I had didn't belong to me.

They locked me up for a few hours and then took me to court. The judge gave me two months in prison for what I did, and they took me to a prison in Arizona. Within fifteen days of being there, I was transferred to another jail, but when they came to get me, I was so upset that I fainted.

When I got to the other prison, they asked me if I wanted to work in the prison kitchen in exchange for phone privileges. I worked eight hours a day slicing meat like ham, salami, and pastrami. When I told my parents that I was working, they got very worried and said that sort of job was too strenuous for me. Whenever I spoke with them, I knew that all my conversations were being recorded. My mom was so sad that she couldn't stop crying every day because of what I was going through.

When they realized I was a minor, the guards put me in solitary confinement, separated from the rest of the women. I felt that I was going to die of loneliness. All day long I cried because I was scared that something would happen to me in that freezing room with no windows. It was too silent and smelled like the antiseptics used in hospitals. I never had an appetite. The food there was totally bland.

Immigration finally picked me up, but when I got to their office, they said that they couldn't set me free yet, because I was a minor and could get hurt. My social worker asked me if I had any siblings in New York who could help me out, and my sister-in-law ended up doing my paperwork. My social worker sent her the forms to fill out, which then had to be sent to Washington for my case.

The day that everything was finally resolved was very dear to me. It was the day I got to New York, and the day I turned 18. I started a new life as an adult in a completely new place. My siblings hugged me when I arrived. Now I'm really happy here living with them. Every weekend we have get-togethers. We talk about soccer when Mexico is playing or we play lotto. We eat mole and pozole.

Now that I'm in New York, I want to work hard to help my parents escape the poverty they're living in. I like studying and working towards my career. I'd like to be a kindergarten teacher one day because I really like being around little kids; they're cute and cuddly.

Even though I'm happy now, what happened to me when I first got to this country was very hard. Coming to the United States is hard for all us immigrants who try to cross the border with so much effort in search of a better life and a good future for our relatives. I wouldn't want anyone else to suffer the way I did.

¿Cómo Te Sentirías al Estar en Una Cárcel?

Sindy
Mexico

Cuando yo decidí venir a los Estados Unidos desde México, yo crucé la frontera en carro con una visa falsa. Me puse muy nerviosa y tenía mucho miedo cuando inmigración me pidió la visa. Después me dijeron que me bajara del carro. Me hicieron preguntas y después me llevaron a su oficina porque se dieron cuenta que yo no era la de la visa.

Me encerraron unas horas y después me llevaron a corte con el juez. Me dio 2 meses de cárcel por haber cruzado con la visa falsa y me llevaron a una cárcel en Arizona. A los 15 días me cambiaron a otra cárcel, pero cuando me iban a cambiar, me desmayé del susto.

Cuando llegué a la otra cárcel me dijeron que si quería trabajar en la cocina y a cambio nos daban una tarjeta para poder hablar por teléfono. Trabajaba 8 horas al día cortando carne como jamón, salami, y pastrami. Cuando yo les dije a mis papás que trabajaba, se preocuparon mucho y me dijeron que ese trabajo no era para mí por que era muy pesado. Cuando yo hablaba con ellos por teléfono a México, la cárcel grababa todas mis conversaciones. Mi mamá se la pasaba llorando todo los días por lo que me estaba pasando a mí y se preocupaba mucho.

Cuando se dieron cuenta que yo tenia 17 años, me metieron en un cuarto solo, separada de los adultos. Sentí que me iba a morir porque me desapartaron de todas las personas. Me sentía muy mal todos los días y me la pasaba llorando porque tenía miedo que me pasara algo porque era un cuarto sin ventanas y muy frió. Olía como un hospital, como a cloro y estaba todo en silencio profundo. Cuando me llevaban de comer no quería comer nada. Las comidas que le daban a uno estaban muy feas—desabridas, sin sal, sin sabor a nada.

Inmigración me recogió, pero cuando llegué a su oficina me dijeron que no me iban a sacar porque las personas me podían hacer daño. Mi trabajadora social me preguntó si tenía hermanos aquí en New York para que me ayudaran, y mi cuñada me ayudó. Le mandaron un paquete de papeles para que ella los rellenara y los mandara a mi trabajadora social. Luego ella mandó los papeles a Washington para que aprobaran mi caso.

El día se solucionó todo y salí del albergué fue un día muy especial porque ese día cumplí mis 18 años y empecé una nueva etapa. Me convertí en adulto y empecé una vida nueva en New York. Mis hermanos me abrazaron cuando llegué. Ahora estoy muy contenta aquí conviviendo con mis hermanos. Todos los fines de semana nos llevamos de maravilla en las fiestas, todos juntos.

Conversamos sobre el futbol cuando juega México y jugamos la lotería. Saboreamos el mole y el pozole cuando lo están cocinando.

Ahora que estoy en New York me gusta trabajar mucho para poder sacar a mis padres de la pobreza en la que están. Me gusta estudiar mucho y tener una carrera. Algún día me gustaría ser educadora de jardín de niños porque me llaman mucho la atención los niños pequeños porque son muy lindos y cariñosos.

Aunque ahora estoy feliz, lo que me pasó cuando llegué a este país fue una experiencia muy dura. Venir a los Estados Unidos es muy difícil para todos los inmigrantes que intentamos cruzar la frontera con tanto esfuerzo para buscar una vida mejor y tener un buen futuro para sus familiares. No me gustaría que ningún inmigrante sufra como lo que yo sufrí.

My Dedication to Studying

Henry Cepin
Dominican Republic

They call me Cepin, my last name, out of love. When I was little, I spent nine years studying in the United States, and I got the chance to do a lot of things. Then, we moved to the Dominican Republic, and I just came back. But when I got to my country, I had a lot of problems with my Spanish. I didn't know much, and when I got to a certain grade, they placed me in a lower one. When I reached the eighth grade for the national exams that they always do in the Dominican Republic, I felt weird because all of my friends were in a higher grade. They were in their junior or senior year of high school.

When I saw that my friends were ahead of me, I felt bad that people might think I was two years behind. It was one of those situations where I felt awkward, and I realized people might think I do nothing but sleep. I had to realize what was going on because I heard rumors that I was a loser. That affected me a lot and I felt bad. And so I realized I had to study!

What happened is that when I lived here, I knew a lot of English. But over there, people don't like it when you speak English, because they can't understand it. So I always spoke Spanish. When I lived there with my mother, my family and everyone else spoke to me in Spanish, so my English suffered. Now is when I need English more than ever, and I am having difficulty speaking it. The little English I know is from long ago. Now I have the hardest time with writing. When you practice something, it helps you a lot, but I never practiced speaking or writing; I did everything in Spanish.

My brothers are all professionals in Santo Domingo. I am the youngest in my family, but I want to be a professional as well. I don't want my family to talk about me and say, "You went over there, we gave you everything when you were a child, and you didn't take advantage of it." And you see, things like that stay in my head. My mother put us in high school in the Dominican Republic, but I didn't devote myself to studying because of my problem with the language. I want my family to see that this kid came here and made something of himself. He dedicated himself to studying and didn't come here to lose himself like a lot of people, a lot of Dominicans, and a lot of people from other countries who come here. One has to focus on what one wants to be, and then everything can be done in this life. You know that you always have to do things the right way so you will reach your goals. If you do things the right way, you'll succeed no matter what. Some people dedicate themselves to money and become drug dealers. You won't get far doing that. If you dedicate yourself to studying for a period of time, the benefits will come later. I have really dedicated myself to studying, and look who I am now.

My Youth in the Dominican Republic
When I lived in the Dominican Republic, I had a cousin who played baseball, and now he's here on the Chicago White Sox. I grew up playing with him over there in Santo Domingo and played ball on a team with him in school. I got to go to other countries to play and to represent the Dominican Republic. I got to come here, to Venezuela, and to Puerto Rico when I was in high school. I was playing well. I was being checked out to sign with a team.

I felt really good because I went to Venezuela and Puerto Rico with my mom and dad. They went to see my games during those times and when I lived here, too. When I was nine years old, I also played here in school. But in Santo Domingo, I really dedicated myself to baseball. When you're really into a sport, you can't hang out and do everything you want. It's difficult and you just live for the sport; you wake up, go to train, and sometimes at three you take classes, and from there, you go to bed. I was given classes, but about baseball. You can't go out much. You just can't. Over there, when you're in the special training school, you can't go out. You can only dedicate yourself to what you are doing.

Sometimes I really liked it, and the people from my country still call. They ask if I'm playing and my dad tells them yes, that I am playing. But I feel disappointed, because my arm just isn't the same. I haven't played now for about three years. One time I was playing and I slid into second base. I fractured my left arm and they took me to the hospital. After that, I couldn't keep playing. Because I was so into baseball and had made it big, you can imagine how bad I felt after this happened.

I want to have a profession, because someone who doesn't study right now, in any country, is a nobody. You don't have the same possibilities as someone who studies. The main thing I want is to help my family. I want my family to see me move forward. Because when I came over here, my mom told me, "Dedicate yourself to your studies and do not get into things. In the United States there are a lot of boys and the majority lose themselves here in this country."

Thanks for reading my story.

Mi Dedicación en los Estudios

Henry Cepin
Dominican Republic

Me dicen Cepin, mi apellido y me lo dicen de cariño. Cuando yo estaba pequeño, yo duré 9 años estudiando en los Estados Unidos y yo llegué a hacer muchas cosas. Después nos mudamos para la Republica Dominicana. Me fui para allá y ahora regresé para acá otra vez. Pero cuando llegué a mi país tenía muchos problemas con el español. No sabía mucho y cuando llegué a un grado, me tuvieron que poner en un nivel más básico. Cuando llegué a octavo curso, para las pruebas nacionales que allá siempre hacen, yo me sentía raro porque todos mis amigos estaban en curso alto. Ellos estaban ya en cuarto de bachillerato o en tercero.

Cuando yo veía los amigos míos que estaban más altos que yo, yo me sentía mal que me bajaron dos años. Eso fue una de las situaciones que a mí me dio cosa. Yo veo hoy en día que esas personas que no se dedican a nada, dizque a dormir y eso….Uno tiene que primero enfilarse porque yo cogí como una noticia que yo me quedé. Eso me afecto mucho a mí y yo me sentía muy mal. Entonces me di cuenta que uno tiene que estudiar.

Lo que pasa es que cuando yo vivía aquí yo sabía mucho inglés. Allá las personas no les gusta que tú hables en inglés porque no saben inglés. Yo me la vivía hablando español. Entonces cuando yo vivía allá con mi madre, mi familia y todo el mundo me hablaban español. Entonces ahora es que yo lo necesito más el inglés y ahora tengo dificultad con eso. Ahora tengo más dificultad para la escritura. Cuando uno practica una cosa, eso te ayuda mucho pero yo nunca practicaba y yo hacía todo en español.

Los hermanos míos son toditos profesionales allá en Santo Domingo. Yo soy el más pequeño de mi familia pero yo quiero ser profesional también. Yo no quiero que la familia me anden hablando que, "Tú te fuiste allá, te dimos todo cuando eras chiquito y tú no aprovechaste tu tiempo." Y tú ves cosas así y eso me llega a la mente. Mi mamá me puso en grande colegio en la Republica Dominicana pero no me dedique a estudiar por mi problema. Quiero que la familia vea que ese niño vino aquí y mira quién es él ahora. Se dedicó al estudio y no vino aquí a perderse como vienen mucha gente, mucho dominicanos, muchas personas de muchos países que vienen. Esto no puedo hacer. Uno tiene que enfocarse en lo que uno quiere llegar y todo se puede en esta vida. Tú sabes que siempre tienes que hacerlo bien hecho y como quiera tú llegas. Si tú lo haces bien hecho tú llegas como quiera, tú llegas. Tú sabes que algunas personas se dedican al dinero, a traficar drogas. Esos no llegan lejos. Tú sabes, uno se dedica al estudio por un tiempo pero después hay beneficios. Yo me dediqué mucho al estudio y mira quien soy ahora.

Mi Juventud en la Republica Dominicana
Yo cuando vivía en la República Dominicana tenía un primo que jugaba béisbol y está aquí en los Chicago White Sox. Yo vivía jugando con él allá en Santo Domingo y estaba en la escuela con él jugando pelota. Sin embargo, yo llegué a ir a otros países a jugar y a representar a la República Dominicana. Llegué a venir acá, a Venezuela, y a Puerto Rico cuando estaba en la secundaria. Yo estaba jugando bien. Ya me estaban chequeando para dedicarme a un equipo.

Yo me sentí muy bien porque fui a Venezuela y a Puerto Rico con mi papá y mi mamá. Fueron a ver mis juegos en esos tiempos y también cuando yo vivía aquí. Cuando tenía nueve años, yo jugaba también aquí en la escuela. Pero en Santo Domingo yo me estaba dedicando mucho a la pelota. Uno cuando esta así no puede salir y hacer esto o lo otro. Es difícil y uno nada más vivía…uno se levantaba, se iba así a entrenarse y a veces a las 3 tomaba clase. Te dan clase pero de béisbol y de ahí, para tu cama. No puedes estar saliendo mucho. No puedes. Allá cuando tú estás en la escuela, no puedes salir. Tú nada más te tienes que dedicar a lo que tú estas haciendo.

A veces me gustaba mucho y todavía me llaman la gente de mi país. Le preguntan a mi papá que si yo estoy jugando y él dice que sí, que yo estoy. Pero yo me desilusioné porque con este brazo ya no es lo mismo. Yo ya tengo como 3 años que no juego. Una vez yo estaba jugando en el play y me tiré en la segunda base. Me fracturé el brazo izquierdo y me llevaron para el hospital. Entonces de ahí no pude seguir jugando. Como me gustaba tanto el béisbol y llegué a algo e iba todo bien en Santo Domingo, imagínate como me sentí después que me pasó esto.

Yo quiero hacer una profesión porque el que no estudia ahora mismo, en cualquier país, no es nadie. Sino que no tiene las mismas posibilidades de cualquier persona que estudia. Yo lo único que quiero es ayudar a mi familia, y que la familia de uno vea que uno hecha para adelante. Porque cuando yo venía para acá, mi mamá me dijo, "Dedícate a tu estudio y no te pongas a estar en cosas. En los Estados Unidos hay muchos muchachos y se pierden la mayoría aquí en este país."

Gracias por leer mi historia.

My Father is the Most Wonderful Person in My Life

Natasha De La Cruz

Dominican Republic

We used to live in Santiago, Dominican Republic. When we were told that we got visas and that we had to be in New York before August 3rd, my mom was very happy, and we had a big party in our house. This summer, I want to go back to my country because I miss it. I like the Dominican Republic because it has a lot of things that I don't have here. I miss my friends. And there, I didn't have to wear so many layers. I wish I were in the Dominican Republic now, because they are celebrating the Dominican Carnival. It's a Dominican tradition. I used to go to the Carnival every Sunday to see the queen. I sometimes feel sad because, there, I used to go out a lot, but here, I just go from school to the apartment to watch TV, do my homework, and then to bed. There, I would get home from school at five-thirty, I would take off my uniform, and I would go out.

I would get back at eight pm, but when I was out my dad would always call me, asking, "Where are you at? Come home." I'd say, "Dad, what do you want?" "For you to make me coffee." I would have to make him coffee, but I've been doing that forever. I've spent my best and my worst times with my dad. When he broke up with his girlfriend, I was the one who cleaned and cooked. I always woke up at six in the morning to make him coffee. He went to work, and he left me at my mom's; we lived far waway from my mom. I always went out with my dad. We'd go fishing, or he'd take me to the beach.

Ever since I was ten years old, I'd tell my dad that I wanted a Quinceañera. Girls always dream about their fifteenth birthday party, the Quince. But it always turns out differently than how we imagined it. My dad opened an account and started to save money for the party when I was twelve. I started to save, but then I lost interest. I took the money out, and I bought my mom a gift for Mother's Day and some things for my dad, too. Later, my dad had to open his checkbook in American dollars and his other one in Dominican pesos to try to put together what we'd need for the party. Finally, the day arrived. My birthday is on March 23rd, but we had the party on Saturday, March 29th, because we didn't have everything ready in time.

That month was really stressful for me, because I had to practice my dance, the waltz, and a choreographed reggaeton dance; I also had to find a dress, the special chair, the crown, and the cake. We filled a bucket with ice to keep the drinks cold. We served rum and beer. My dad bought me a bottle of champagne and a bottle of wine. But my dad didn't dance the waltz with me. I had to ask an uncle to dance with me.

My dad knows everything about me and he buys me the clothes and things I need. For me, my dad is the most wonderful person that I have in life, because I trust him more than anything. I cried a lot when I found out that I would have to leave my people, and most importantly, my dad, behind. I knew that I was going to start over in a new world, very different from the one that I lived in. My life was empty without my dad. Now that I know that he's coming on March 10th, I'm very happy. I feel that happiness has come into my life again.

Mi Papá es Lo Más Maravilloso en Mi Vida

Niza De La Cruz
Dominican Republic

Nosotros vivíamos en Santiago. Cuando nos dijeron que estábamos visados y que teníamos que estar en New York antes del 3 de Agosto, mi mamá se puso contenta y hubo una fiesta grande en casa. En el verano pienso irme a mi país porque lo extraño. Me gusta porque hay muchas cosas que aquí no tengo: extraño a mis amigos y allá no tenía que andar con tantas ropas puestas. Me gusta estar en mi país porque en esta época se celebra el carnaval de los Dominicanos. Es una tradición, yo iba todos los domingos al carnaval a ver a la reina. A veces me siento triste porque allá yo salía mucho pero aquí yo voy desde la escuela al apartamento a sentarme a ver televisión, hago mi tarea, y a la cama. Pero allá yo llegaba de mi escuela a la 5 y media, me quitaba el uniforme y me iba a andar.

Volvía a las 8 de la noche pero mi papá se mantenía llamándome "¿Dónde tú está? Ven para acá." Yo iba, "Papi ¿qué tú quiere?" "Que me cuele un café." Tenía que ponerme a colar café pero esa costumbre es de siempre. Yo estaba en los peores y mejores momentos con mi papá. Cuando el se dejaba de su mujer, era yo la que le lavaba, cocinaba. Me levantaba a las 6 de la mañana a colarle su café. Él se iba a trabajar y me llevaba donde mi mamá porque vivíamos un poco retirados de mi mamá. Yo siempre salía con mi papá. Me iba con él de pesca o me llevaba a playa.

Desde que tenía 10 años le decía a mi papá que quería mi fiesta de 15. Las jóvenes siempre soñamos con nuestros 15. Pintamos la fiesta de una manera pero nos sale de otra. Mi papá me abrió una cuenta y empecé a juntar dinero para la fiesta a los 12. Comencé a ahorrar pero después me desencanté. Saqué mi dinero y le compré un regalo a mi mamá para el Día de la Madre y cosas que le di a mi papá. Después mi papá abrió su libreta en dólares y en pesos dominicanos y comenzó a juntar para cuando llegara ese día. Cuando llegó ese día, mi cumpleaños es el 23 de Marzo, me lo hicieron un Sábado 29 de Marzo porque no teníamos todo preparado.

Ese fue un mes muy agitado para mí, porque tenía que ensayar el baile, mi vals, el baile de reggaeton y también tuve que buscar el vestido y la silla, la corona, y el biscocho. Llenamos un tanque con hielo para echar las bebidas para que no se calienten. Se dio ron, cerveza. Mi papá me compró una botella de champaña y una de vino. Pero mi papá no bailó el vals conmigo. Tuve que buscar un tío mío para eso.

Mi papá sabe todo de mí; me compraba mis ropas y cosas. Para mí, papá es lo más maravilloso que tengo en la vida porque en él he depositado toda mi confianza. Lloré mucho al saber que dejaba a mi gente y principalmente a mi padre. Yo sabía que iba a empezar en un mundo muy diferente al que yo vivía. Era muy vacía la vida sin la presencia de mi padre. Ahora al saber que el viene el 10 de marzo me siento muy feliz. Siento que de nuevo llegó la felicidad a mi vida.

The New Revolution

Arafat La Leyenda
Honduras

Have you ever been into something bad and promised to change? I have been here in the United States for about four months, and nothing is easy. For example, the language, getting to know the city, and above all, learning how to relate to people are all difficult; here and everywhere, people are not the same. Here, in the United States, not everyone understands your language. When they hear you speaking a language that they do not understand, they think that you are talking about them, and they stare at you, looking for reasons to start a problem. But I know that I can do things the right way.

I have an objective here while I'm in school, and it is to learn English and to succeed. If I know how to speak English, it becomes easier to get a job, and I can converse with other people. I study for one hour every day after I get out of school. I have friends who speak English, and I try to speak with them.

Recently, in Honduras, everything that went through my head concerned joining a gang, and it was nothing good. People were fighting and causing problems—the type of problems that in reality are fighting with fists and dishing out blows. The thing was that the problems weren't only with me. My mother became ill when she heard I was in trouble. Later, my mother told my father about what I was doing and all of that caused a problem, because my relationship with people was different.

With my actions, people only stared at me, and it was only when I was with my family that they spoke to me. I spoke with those I considered to be my second family, my friends from the gang. I told myself that I couldn't continue doing those things. I couldn't because I always have to think about my mother and myself, because I have a lot ahead of me. I knew that what I was doing was wrong, and at one point, I told my mother that I promised to change, and that is what is happening now.

There are many people in the world who migrate from one country to the next without having goals, and the best thing they feel they can do is join a gang. I know a friend who came to the United States without a goal and made that decision. Because of that, he has been in jail and has caused his mother many problems. She had to give him money and buy him everything he wanted, because while in the prison, he didn't have the option to work and this became a weight on his mother's shoulders. She had other sons who were younger and she had to watch them carefully. And his mother, it's all up to her, because she doesn't live with the father of her children. She is both mother and father to her children. This is something that I have always thought about—that the mother is the only one, and she does not deserve to suffer for the bad things that her children do.

La Nueva Revolución

Arafat La Leyenda
Honduras

¿Alguna vez has estado en algo malo y has prometido cambiar? Tengo como cuatro meses aquí en los Estados Unidos pero no es nada fácil. Por ejemplo, el idioma, el conocimiento de la ciudad y sobre todo, aprender a relacionarse con las personas porque aquí y en todas partes, las personas no son iguales. Aquí en los Estados Unidos, no todos entienden tu idioma. Cuando ellos te escuchan hablando un idioma que no entienden, ellos piensan que tú estás hablando de ellos y te quedan viendo más, buscando motivos para formar un problema. Pero yo sé que puedo hacerlo bien.

Tengo un propósito estando aquí en la escuela que es aprender bien el inglés y salir adelante. Si yo sé hablar el inglés, tengo más facilidad de tener un trabajo y poder dialogar con otras personas. Yo estudio una hora todos los días después que salgo de la escuela. Tengo amigos que hablan en inglés y trato de hablar con ellos.

Recientemente, en Honduras, todo lo que pasaba por mi cabeza era meterme en una ganga y no era nada bueno. Las personas tenían que pelear y enfrentar problemas. Ese tipo de problemas que en verdad es pelear con puños, dando golpes. La cosa es que el problema no era solo para mí. Mi mamá se ponía mal cuando escuchaba que yo estaba en problemas. Luego mi mamá le decía a mi papa que era lo que yo estaba haciendo y todo eso porque ya mi relación con las personas era diferente.

Yo con mis actuaciones, la gente solo me quedaban viendo y solo con mi familia me hablaban. Yo hablaba con los que yo consideraba mi segunda familia que eran mis amigos de la ganga. Yo me dije que no puedo seguir haciendo estas cosas. No puedo porque siempre tengo que pensar en mi mamá y en mí porque yo tengo mucho por delante. Yo sabia que las cosas que estaba haciendo no estaban bien y hubo un momento que yo le dije a mi mamá que prometo cambiar y eso yo se que esta pasando.

Existen muchas personas en el mundo que emigran de un país a otro sin tener metas y lo mejor que pueden hacer es meterse en una ganga. Yo conozco a un amigo que llegó a los Estados Unidos sin tener una meta y tomo esa decisión. Por eso, él ha estado preso y ha metido a la mamá en problemas. Tuvo que darle dinero y comprarle todo lo que quiere porque estando en el precinto, no tiene la opción de trabajar y es un peso para la mamá porque ella tiene otros hijos que son más pequeños y tiene que ponerle cuidado. Y la mamá, solo es ella porque no vive con el papá de sus hijos. Ella es madre y padre para sus hijos. Eso es algo que yo siempre he estado pensando. En que la madre solo hay una y ella no se merece sufrir por las cosas malas que los hijos hacen.

Fighting for a Dream

Adrian Gonzalez
Guatemala

Have you ever given up on your dreams because of a problem you couldn't overcome? Well, this almost happened to me.

My parents simply couldn't afford to provide us with everything we needed. My family is very large, but I didn't have anyone to share my childhood with because my parents were always arguing over money. During my entire childhood, I hoped that my parents would stop arguing and start giving us some love. But whenever I woke up from these dreams, all I had was emptiness in my heart.

When I was eight, I realized that I had to get a job if I wanted to keep studying at the national school, because my parents couldn't help me. I started working in construction six hours a day after school, but work was so tiring that I often fell asleep in class. The years went by filled with disappointments and without the moral and economic support I needed. There were times when I didn't even have clothes to wear. In the end, I kept going because of someone who gave me strength—one of my siblings, the one dearest to me. He's much older than I and has never been able to walk or speak. He was the reason I kept going.

One day, I came home and saw him sitting in the backyard. I started thinking about my life and about his. I realized that I had two things he didn't have that allowed me to do things he only dreamt about. Those two things would have let him fight against all odds and achieve what he wanted. After this long reflection, I realized that I wasn't lacking anything physically. What I was missing was inner strength—the will and self-confidence to face all that kept me from achieving what I want. Thinking this through left me both strong and hurt, because I realized that I had taken many things for granted. In the end, I found the answer I was looking for and kept studying.

Two months before graduation, something came up that destroyed everything I had worked for. It all started one day at school when I found a letter on my desk. I put it in my pocket and headed to the bathroom. I tore the envelope and started to read. What it said left me completely shocked. It asked that I join a group of drug dealers and promised that I would make so much money that I would never have to work or study again. If I refused, they would kill me and my family.

Four days later, I was walking home from school down a quiet street when four guys wearing ski masks grabbed me. One of them asked me what choice I had made, but I told him that they were wasting their time because I preferred to die. As I finished answering, the one who had asked me punched me in the face and said, "Don't you realize what this means for you and your family?" Luckily, five of my schoolmates were walking down the street, so the men let me go and ran away. But the one who had punched me told me to reconsider, and as he did, he cut me across my stomach twice. My face and my stomach were bleeding as I headed home to treat my injuries.

That night I thought about the serious danger that I was putting my family in, and the only way out was equally as difficult. I planned a long trip that would endanger my life. I told my mother that I would move to the States to keep my family from being killed. It wasn't easy because I had to borrow a lot of money and knew that I'd really miss my family, especially my mom. On the other hand, I knew what would happen if I stayed.

Nearly two months later, we were taking our final exams to find out if we could move on to the next grade. It was a Wednesday. I headed to school to find out if I had passed. But as I walked into my classroom, I found a letter in the same spot where the other one had been. It said that I'd be killed if I didn't change my mind. Then the principal started to read out our grades. I had passed.

I dreaded walking home that day, knowing that it would be the last night I slept at home. I packed my bags for my trip and tried to sleep, but I couldn't stop thinking of what would happen to me during my journey. Before I knew it, my parents were knocking on my door to wake me up. As I said goodbye to everyone, especially my mom, I felt a knot in my throat but couldn't cry. I got in the car with the man who was taking me to the Mexican border.

The first four days weren't that bad, but on the fifth we started walking non-stop. That's the day I realized that every step I took was a step farther away from my family. I ate only one meal that day and that's how it always was until I got to the border. When I got to the States, I walked for another five days with no food or sleep, feeling cold and thirsty until I got to the place where I took a bus to New York.

When I first got here and had to leave the house to get food, I was terrified because I didn't know anyone. I didn't even know how to say "Hi." But after a few months I started to overcome my fears. I won't stop fighting for my dreams.

Luchando Por un Sueño

Adrian Gonzalez

Guatemala

¿Alguna vez te has rendido ante un problema que te impide luchar para realizar tus sueños? Porque a mí casi me pasó eso.

Mis padres no podían brindarnos lo necesario. En mi familia somos muchos, pero no tenía una persona con quien compartir el papel de un niño y mis padres se mantenían peleando porque no tenían dinero para las cosas que necesitamos. Durante toda mi niñez, soñaba que mis padres dejaran de pelear y que nos dieran un poco de amor a mis hermanos y a mí. Pero cuando terminaba de soñar, lo único que me dejaba era un vacío en mi corazón.

Cuando tenía 8 años vi la necesidad de conseguir un trabajo para poder estudiar en la escuela nacional del estado porque mis padres no podían ayudarme. Empecé a trabajar para un señor en construcción por seis horas después de la escuela, pero el trabajo era tan pesado que hubieron tantas veces que me dormí en el salón de clases. Así pasaron los años, con decepciones, sin ayuda moral o ayuda económica. Muchas veces hasta me faltó el vestuario adecuado. Pero al final hubo alguien que me dio la fuerza para seguir—uno de mis hermanos, el más especial en mi vida. El es mucho mayor que yo y creció sin poder caminar ni hablar. Sin embargo, él fue para mi vida como una fuente porque yo iba a dejar de estudiar.

Un día llegué a la casa y lo vi a él sentado en el patio y pensé muchas cosas sobre mi vida y su vida. Me di cuenta que yo tengo dos cosas que mi hermano no tiene que me permiten hacer mucho. Quizás él deseé luchar con todas las circunstancias que se le presenten en la vida y al fin lograr lo que quiere y lo que se propone tener. Al final de esa reflexión que tuve, me di cuenta que no me hacía falta nada físicamente. Lo que me hacía falta era algo en mi interior, la seguridad y voluntad en mi mismo para enfrentar todas las cosas que me impiden hacer algo en mi vida. Me dejó una fuerza y a la vez un dolor porque entendí que yo estaba desperdiciando mucho. Al final hallé la respuesta en mí mismo para empezar el nivel básico.

Cuando faltaban dos meses por terminar todo ese nivel de 4 años, otro problema llegó para destruir todo lo que había logrado. En mi colegio encontré una carta sobre mi escritorio. La guardé en mi bolsa del pantalón, me fui al baño, entré y abrí el sobre para leerla. Al terminar, me dejó muy impresionado. Me pedía que formara parte de un grupo que trafica droga. También decía que al vender yo tendría mucho dinero sin trabajar ni estudiar, pero también decía que si no lo aceptaba, que se encargarían en destruirme y a mi familia también.

Después de cuatro días, salí del colegio. Iba caminando por una calle silenciosa, cuando de repente aparecieron cuatro hombres con la cara cubierta con pasamontañas. Dos de los tres me agarraron y el otro se paró en frente de mí. Me preguntó sobre la propuesta, pero yo le respondí que habían perdido su tiempo conmigo porque preferiría morir antes de aceptar. Al terminar de decir esto, el que estaba pasando en frente de mí me dio tres golpes en la cara y me dijo, "¿Sabes que estás sentenciando tu vida y la de tu familia?" De casualidad cinco estudiantes del mismo colegio venían caminando por la misma calle. Los hombres me soltaron y me dijeron al final que yo lo pensara bien. Empezaron a correr, pero el que estuvo parado frente de mi me rozó el estómago dos veces con la navaja. Cuando llegaron los cinco estudiantes yo estaba sangrando mucho por la cara y el estómago. Me fui a la casa para curarme las heridas.

En esa noche pensé sobre el peligro que podrían enfrentar cada uno de mi familia y la única solución que encontré para protegerlos fue una decisión difícil. Pensé hacer un viaje muy largo donde tenía que arriesgar mi vida. Le dije a mi mamá que yo quería ir a los Estados Unidos para no poner en riesgo la vida de cada uno de mis hermanos. No fue fácil porque tuve que pedir prestado mucho dinero para el viaje y también porque no era fácil para mí alejarme de mis hermanos y principalmente me madre. Por otro lado sabía lo que me iba a pasar si no me iba.

Paso otro mes y veinte días. Era la última semana del colegio y estábamos haciendo los exámenes finales para saber si íbamos a ser promovidos.

Era un miércoles. Fui al colegio por mis resultados. Entré a mi salón de clases y sobre mi escritorio, en el mismo lugar, encontré otro sobre. Empecé a leer y decía lo mismo—me amenazaba de muerte si rechazaba de nuevo. El director empezó a darnos los resultados. Yo había sido promovido.

Regresé a mi casa con un vació en mi corazón porque era el ultimo día que podía dormir en mi casa. En la noche guardé mi ropa para el viaje y después intenté dormir pero no podía porque pensaba en lo que me esperaba en el transcurso del viaje. Mi mamá y mi papá tocaron la puerta para decirme que ya era hora de comenzar el viaje. Cuando me despedía de cada uno de ellos, principalmente de mi mama, sentía un nudo en la garganta pero no podía llorar. Me entré en un carro con el señor que me iba a dejar en la frontera con México.

Los primeros cuatro días de viaje no fueron difíciles pero después el quinto día caminamos sin parar. Ese día comprendí que cada paso que yo daba era la distancia que yo me estaba alejando de mi familia. Ese día comí solo una vez y así pasaban todos los días hasta llegar a la frontera. Después de cruzarla, caminé cinco días sin comer ni dormir sintiendo frió y sed hasta llegar al lugar donde tomé un bus a New York.

Cuando llegué aquí, salía a comprar la comida con miedo porque no conocía a nadie ni sabia como saludar a una persona. Pero después de unos meses el miedo que yo tenía lo empecé a superar. Hoy no dejo de luchar por mis sueños.

My Passion for Baseball

David

Dominican Republic

I moved to New York in 2008, and I've only been here for a year and four months. It was a big change for me and a big surprise. But it wasn't a good surprise; I had to move here right away because my father got sick. We had just received our visas, and a few days later he had a stroke in the Dominican Republic. My mom had to bring him here, and I had to stay behind with my little brother for 21 days. I was seventeen and he was thirteen, and we were with our other sisters who are still over there. My brother and I spent all our time playing in the streets to forget what we were going through.

In the Dominican Republic, I used to play baseball, but when I moved here, I had a hard time at first, because I couldn't find a team. When I was in Albany, I played on a high school team. It was boring in Albany, and no one spoke Spanish, so my mom decided to move us to the city. But I think that my little brother and I would've learned English faster there. I learned so much while I lived there, because everyone at my school spoke English exclusively. That made it hard when it was time to play baseball. Because I barely spoke English, I had to imagine what my coach was telling me to do during the game. I was able to follow along not because of my language skills but because of my years of experience in the sport.

When I was back in my country, I played in a really important home match between Puerto Rico and the Dominican Republic. It was such a momentous event in my life; there were tons of fans watching me. My coach had said during practice, "David, you're going to be the first one to pitch." I didn't let my team down, thank God. Even though we lost the game, everyone complimented me on how well I played.

My mom has taught me to treat people nicely and respectfully. She's shown me that I shouldn't look for trouble or do anything bad. I am the way that I am today because of the way she raised me. She has always supported my dreams of playing in the big leagues and paid for fees and equipment for every team I've been a part of. She's always in the crowd, watching me at every game, checking to see how I'm improving. I think that everyone wants to win at baseball. One of my greatest goals is to make it to the big leagues, and I hope to make it one day. Nothing's impossible. If you want to make it big in baseball, don't let simple things like the climate get in your way. After a while, you get used to it. At least, that's what my mother has taught me.

La Pasión Por el Baseball

David
Dominican Republic

Yo vine aquí a New York en el 2008 de la Republica Dominicana y solo tengo un año y 4 meses que vine de mi país. Yo vine aquí de sorpresa. Bueno, no fue de sorpresa porque mi papá se enfermó. Le dio un derrame cerebral allá en la Republica Dominicana y lo tuvieron que traer, y mi mamá tuvo que venir con él de emergencia. Mi papá se enfermó como a la semana de darnos la visa para venir a los Estados Unidos a mi hermano, a mi mamá y a mí. Entonces mi mamá vino después de esa semana. Yo tuve que durar 21 días con mi hermano de 13 años, pero yo, en ese tiempo, tenía 17 años. Mi hermano y yo nos quedamos con dos hermanas más que yo tengo, que se tuvieron que quedar en la Republica Dominicana. Y mi hermano y yo, desde que mi mamá no estaba con nosotros, siempre estábamos jugando en las calles para olvidarnos un poco de lo que estaba pasando, y para que los días se pasaran más rápido.

Para mí fue una experiencia muy grande porque en la Republica Dominicana yo jugaba béisbol, y con el cambio de venir para acá, no encontraba en qué equipo ponerme a jugar. El año pasado yo estaba jugando en high school en Albany. Ya que allá no hablaban el español y era muy aburrido, mi mamá decidió mudarnos a una ciudad donde se habla español. Pero yo creo que para mí y para mi hermano menor nos convenía quedarnos allá para aprender inglés. Lo poquito que yo sé lo he aprendido allá, porque en la escuela en Albany no había nadie que hablaba en español.

Eso era un problema porque yo estaba en el equipo de béisbol y como no sabía tanto inglés, yo tenía que imaginarme la instrucciones con la experiencia que yo tenía jugando béisbol. Cuando un manager me decía una instrucción, yo no me la sabía porque sabía inglés, sino por experiencia más o menos de lo que yo sé.

Yo me acuerdo de un juego importante donde Puerto Rico y Republica Dominicana nos enfrentamos en el terreno del juego en Republica Dominicana, y ese juego fue importante para mí porque fue un evento muy grande. Había muchas personas esperando el día. Y me alegré un día de practica donde el manager me dijo, "David tú vas abrir el juego contra Puerto Rico" y yo le dije que yo estaba bien para pichar. Bueno llegó la hora del juego y gracias a Dios pude hacer mi trabajo como abridor. Aunque perdimos el juego, todos me dijeron que hice un buen trabajo como un picher abridor.

Mi mamá me ha dado esa oportunidad de que yo me pueda relacionar con las demás personas sin ofender, sin buscar problemas, ni comportarme mal con nadie. Por eso es que yo soy como soy, por la disciplina que ella me ha dado. Ella también me apoyaba en mi deseo, que es jugar en las grandes ligas y me pagaba en los equipos que yo he estado. Siempre ella va al play a verme jugar para ver como yo estoy jugando y a ver que tanto estoy progresando en el béisbol. Yo pienso que el béisbol es un juego que todo el mundo quiere ganar. Llegar a las grandes ligas es una de mis metas de mi vida que yo me he propuesto, y espero algún día cumplirla, ya que nada es imposible en la vida. Yo pienso que si usted quiere jugar béisbol no le de importancia al clima, ya que me he dado cuenta que con el tiempo uno se acostumbra al clima y se olvida de cosas tan simples como esa. Bueno, eso es lo que me ha enseñado mi madre.

The Child of God

Chiquito
Dominican Republic

Have you ever known anyone with an illness? I was born with a disease that first started showing its symptoms when I was three years old. I had epileptic seizures until I was twelve years old. Then, I didn't have any more seizures. The doctors say that they won't come back, and it seems to be true because I haven't been sick since. But, because of that illness, I had to go to a special school in Santo Domingo. It wasn't a normal school, because I had learning problems. It wasn't until now pretty much, at eighteen years old, that I am developing.

I am from a neighborhood called Venezuela in Santo Domingo. My friends call me Chiquito, out of love. My dad has a grocery store in Santo Domingo. One day, he got sick and he had to have two operations. They took a bone out of his leg and transplanted it in the back of his neck when they took out a hernia. But they opened him up in the front of his neck. He's okay now. On that same day, my older brother, who helped me out at the grocery store, had a motorcycle accident. So, I became the one who took care of everything in the house.

I went to school, but it wasn't the same. I understood everything in class, but I didn't pay attention because I had other problems to worry about. I ran the grocery store from when I was twelve years old until I turned 18. It was my responsibility. I have a sister, but she's married and she lived on the other side of the city. My brother couldn't help me because of the accident, but together anything is achievable.

I've been living in the Bronx for two months now. Once I finish this program, I'm going to study in another school to become a lawyer. I would like to be a lawyer, because I think the work would be interesting. I hope that when people read my story, it can serve as a lesson that together, anything in the world can be accomplished.

El Niño de Dios

Chiquito
Dominican Republic

¿Has conocido una persona con una enfermedad? Yo cuando nací, a los tres años estaba enfermo. Me convulsionaba hasta los 12 años. Después, a los 12 años, ya se me quitó y no me ha vuelto a dar más nunca. Los doctores decían que era hasta los 12 años y parece que sí porque yo no estuve más enfermo. Pero, por esa enfermedad, yo tenía que estar en una escuela especial en Santo Domingo. No era una escuela igual porque yo tenía problemas de aprendizaje. Ahora es que yo, más o menos, me estoy desarrollando a los 18 años.

Yo soy de la Venezuela en Santo Domingo y mis amigos me dicen Chiquito. Mis amigos me dicen Chiquito de cariño. Mi papá tiene un colmado en Santo Domingo y un día, mi papá cayó enfermo y tuvieron que hacerle dos operaciones. Le sacaron un hueso de la pierna y le dieron un transplante. Se la pusieron ahí atrás, en el cuello, cuando le sacaron una hernia. Pero lo abrieron por alante del cuello. El ya está bien. En ese mismo día, el hermano mío que es mayor que yo, que era el que me ayudaba en el colmado, tuvo un accidente en una pasola. Entonces tuve que encargarme de todo en mi casa.

Yo estudiaba pero no era igual. Yo iba a la escuela y entendía todo pero yo no ponía atención porque había problemas en la casa. Yo me encargaba del colmado desde que tenía 12 año hasta los 18. Tuve esa responsabilidad. Yo tengo una hermana pero ella estaba casada y vivía en otro lado. Mi hermano no pudo ayudarme por el accidente pero unidos se puede lograr todo.

Yo tengo dos meses viviendo aquí en el Bronx. Pienso terminar este programa para después estudiar en otra escuela para poder ser abogado. Me gustaría ser abogado porque me llama la atención esa carrera. Espero que cuando lean mi historia, le sirvan de una experiencia y decirle que unidos, todo en el mundo se puede lograr.

Everything I've Been Through

Jacquie
Dominican Republic

In New York, you can have a better life when you try your hardest to get ahead…

I was born in the United States, in New York, but I was raised for ten years during my childhood in the Dominican Republic. I only needed to finish the last year of high school, but then they sent me to the United States. Here there are more possibilities of having a future, more possibilities of realizing your dreams. When my grandmother, cousin, aunt, and mother dropped me off at the airport, they were all crying. They all wished me luck. The photos that I took on that day remind me of the sadness I felt and the scent of the roses my aunt gave me.

New York and Santo Domingo are very different. In Santo Domingo, I have more friends. Here, I have friends, but they aren't like the ones I have over there, friends whom I can really trust. Here, I have friends I say "Hi, how are you?" and "Bye" to. Here, I have more freedom to go out. In the Dominican Republic, it was much more dangerous. I could only go from my house to school. If I went out, I would have to go with a friend or someone I knew, but I couldn't go out by myself. Here, people are kind of mean and they aren't very social. There, most people know one another. Although they can be a bit gossipy, everyone knows everyone, everyone says "Hi," and they worry about each other. Here, everyone is in his or her own world and no one says "Hi" to anyone. If they bump into you, they just say "I'm sorry," and they keep going. There, things are different.

I've been living here for two years now, almost three. I work and go to school. I work at McDonalds in downtown Manhattan, and I go to school at the Bronx Regional High School. I like where I work, but sometimes it feels like I can barely rest on my days off. Going to school and work and then trying to rest is a tiring routine. When I came to New York, I had to start working because I was living with one of my aunts. She's difficult, and my sister and I had to move out. She was always looking for some excuse to make us look bad in front of my uncle, and I had to find another place to live to avoid the problems that she created.

People have said that I could be a model, but I'm not really interested in modeling right now. When I was little, I wanted to study law. Now, I want to study nursing. I want to follow in the footsteps of my grandfather, who was a doctor, and my grandmother, who was a nurse. It's a good profession. I would like to work in pediatrics, with children. I really like children, and I want to learn everything about them. But first, I need to start as a nurse, and then, later, I'll go into pediatrics. Coming to New York has made me grow as a person and my attitude has improved because I've realized what I really want for my present and my future.

I've always been reserved about sharing my life with others. I think you are your own best friend. Be careful about who you surround yourself with, and remember, never stop fighting for your dreams and your goals. You create your own present and future by knowing how much you are worth. I think about my dreams every day. That is what gives me the strength to keep going.

Todo Lo Que He Pasado

Jacquie

Dominican Republic
En Nueva York uno vive mejor cuando tiene ganas de superarle y seguir adelante...

Yo nací en los Estados Unidos, en Nueva York, pero crecí como 10 años en República Dominicana. Solo me faltaba un año para terminar el bachillerato. Me mandaron a los Estados Unidos. Aquí hay más futuro y uno tiene más posibilidades de realizar sus sueños. Cuando mi abuela, mi prima, mi tía, y mi madre me llevaron al aeropuerto, estaban llorando. Todos me deseaban mucha suerte en todo. Las fotos que tengo de ese día me recuerdan la tristeza que sentía y el perfume de las rosas de mi tía.

Hay muchas diferencias entre Nueva York y Santo Domingo. Allá yo tenía más amigos. Aquí yo tengo amigos pero no como los de allá que podía confiar en ellos. Aquí tengo amigos de decirles hola, cómo estás y bye bye. Aquí tengo más libertad de salir. En República Dominicana es más peligroso. Tenía que estar de mi casa al colegio. Si salía era con un amigo o familiar, pero no podía salir sola. Aquí las personas son como medias antipáticas. No son muy sociales. Allá la mayoría de la gente te conoce. Aunque son un poco chismosas, la mayoría te conoce, te saludan, se preocupan por ti. Aquí todo el mundo está en su mundo y no saluda a nadie. Si te pasan a un lado sólo dicen lo siento y se van. Por allá las cosas son diferentes.

Tengo dos años viviendo en Nueva York. Ya casi voy a cumplir tres años. Trabajo y estudio. Yo trabajo en McDonald's, en downtown Manhattan, y estudio en Bronx Regional High School. Me gusta donde trabajo, pero a veces los días que estoy libre casi no descanso porque tengo que ir a la escuela. Después de venir a Nueva York tuve que comenzar a trabajar porque yo vivía con la esposa de un tío mío. Ella era muy complicada y así mi hermana y yo nos tuvimos que mudarnos. Ella siempre buscaba un pretexto para que nosotras quedáramos mal enfrente de mi tío y tuvimos que buscar una habitación para evitar los problemas.

Me han dicho que yo puedo ser modelo, pero ahora mismo no me interesa el modelaje. Cuando era chiquita yo quería estudiar los derechos. Ahora quiero estudiar enfermería. Quiero seguir la secuencia porque mi abuelo es doctor y mi abuela es enfermera. Es una profesión muy bonita. Me gustaría trabajar en pediatría con los niños. Me gustan mucho los niños y me gustaría saber todo sobre ellos. Pero primero quiero comenzar como enfermera para después entrar a la carrera de pediatría.

Aparte de enfermería yo quería estudiar los derechos pero es muy larga esa carrera y hay demasiados abogados. Voy a tener que durar muchísimo estudiando entonces. Ya no voy a estudiar eso, de verdad está muy larga. Pudiera estudiar psicología pero es otra que dura más. Uno tiene que estar lidiando con toda esa gente. Aunque no lo crean, venir para Nueva York me ha hecho crecer más en los sentidos como una persona y en comportamiento en saber que en realidad quiero para mi futuro y presente.

Siempre he sido muy reservada con mis cosas. Pienso que el mejor amigo de uno es uno mismo. Ten cuidado con los que te rodean, y recuerda nunca deje de la luchar por sus sueños y metas. Tú creas tu propio presente y futuro valorándote a ti mismo.

Life in Two Nations

Musa Jobarteh
The Gambia

My name is Musa Jobarteh and I was born in Gambia on April 12th, 1990. I am proud of my country. I lived with my mom and dad until 1995. Then my mom left Gambia and came to the United States of America. I continued to live with my dad and grandmother. I didn't see my mom for fourteen long years. I started school when I was three years old. The first thing they had to teach me was how to say the alphabet and read and write. Then, when I passed grade seven, I went to high school. In high school, I did track and field. The teachers used to take me to Gambia Methodist Academy, where I participated in different track and field events. I ran and did high jump and long jump for the school. The school gave me a scholarship to do all those things.

Right before each race was about to begin, my heart started racing, because I was scared of the other runners who might beat me. The fans watching me made me feel really nervous, too. Once I started running, I felt excited because I felt confident that I would not disappoint my fans. Many girls started to like me, and they often chanted "Musa, Musa, Musa!" as I ran.

Because I was doing very well at that time, a jealous runner from the other team chased me on the way to a training session one time and began to fight with me. My leg was injured during the fight and I couldn't run for the rest of the track season. Everybody was asking me "Why Musa? Why are you not going to run?" I told them that I had injured my leg and I could not run for the season.

Everybody felt bad, and I was upset too, because I was not able to compete for my school.

In high school, I met and fell in love with a girl named Fatou. She liked me because I was a very good athlete, and I liked her, too. She is gorgeous and tall with a good sense of humor and likes to dance. On July 25th, 2009 Fatou gave birth to our daughter on our third anniversary. I love my girlfriend who is the mother of my child. I will never forget her.

On July 16th, 2009, just before the birth of our daughter, I received my American visa. It was one of the happiest days in my life. I went to the American embassy, and after I waited for less than an hour, they called my name and said I had a visa. I was very excited. I knew I would learn English in New York and my life would change. I felt that the United States was one of the best countries and that it would offer me opportunities to have the best life possible with a job in business management.

On August 15th, 2009, I arrived in New York. Since then I have started to see changes in my life. First, I noticed how many more facilities are available than in my hometown. Here, people have so much more access to transportation, recreation, and schools. On October 11th, 2009, I started school in New York. I saw a big difference between school in Gambia and school in the United States. Schools in the United States have more resources than schools in Gambia. For example, in the cafeteria, students get free lunch and breakfast and even free daycare for the babies so the mothers can go to school. Another example is the computer lab where students do GED exams in math and other subjects. In the gym they can play basketball and do exercises. These are some of the reasons why I say the schools in the United States are better than schools in Gambia. The only way schools in Gambia might be better is that in Africa both boys and girls wear uniforms in school. They don't wear jeans or sneakers; the girls don't braid their hair, and they don't wear earrings or jewelry to school. That is better, because sometimes students in the United States do not even come to school because they don't have new sneakers, and clothing becomes too important. That is the only major difference between schools in Gambia and schools in the United States.

My message to the reader is that life is not easy. It has both good and bad. One should make the best out of life's situations no matter where you are in this world. Take advantage of the opportunities that come your way. Life in America seems to be a paradise compared to Gambia. You must love and appreciate the American experience as well as your entire life experience.

Love from Afar, Over the Distance

Veronica Lizardo
Dominican Republic

My story begins in the city of Santo Domingo, in the neighborhood of Sabana Perdida. I lived in this neighborhood for nineteen years with my grandmother, whom I love dearly. When I got to know more about life, I started asking myself why I had never lived with my mother and little sisters. With time, I understood that my mother had enough problems and that there were five of us girls. She had to work hard for us, and I thank God that today I love and respect my mother, Odalis. Keep in mind that there is only one mother in the world for each of us, and one of those mothers is mine.

As the years passed, I dedicated myself a lot to my school, El Colegio de La Rosa. In the final part of my studies in high school, I started realizing what I really wanted for my future—in other words, what profession I wanted to study in college. But then my father came so that I could travel back to the United States with him to live here with him and my siblings. Suddenly, by the end of August 2009, my siblings and I were already here. Everything happened so fast that I couldn't finish my last year of school in my country. Today, I have a lot of dreams that I want to fulfill now that God has given me the opportunity to be in this country to complete my studies more easily.

But in this beautiful story of my life, I also went through difficult times. Every time I speak about this subject, I get really sad. My thoughts drift to those good moments that I experienced with that person and I will never forget him. The most beautiful moments I have lived happened with my boyfriend, because I was with him for nine years until I had to leave to come to New York. When I told the news to my boyfriend, he did not like the idea very much, but ultimately, he understood. As the days passed, my boyfriend and I were very sad because the day I had to leave was approaching. It's not easy to part, at least for me, but one has to be strong to survive.

The saddest day of my life was the day I was in the airport… Wow. I was in a world where loneliness was killing me. I thought that the world was on my shoulders and I couldn't find a way to rid myself from the great pain that I felt upon leaving the people that I loved the most.

Currently, I feel much better. As long as my grandmother, my mother, and my boyfriend are fine, I am happy. For me, it's a privilege to have the family that God has given me. They appreciate me a lot. Family is the most important thing that one has to take care of; now, more than ever, you must have the support of your family.

I say and express these feelings so that the people who have gone through this problem of loving from a distance can have the willpower to keep moving forward. It doesn't matter if you're far from the person whom you love; just keep in mind the importance of that person. Like the saying goes, "Nobody knows what they have until it is lost." I think that if we have hope, everything we set our minds to, we can accomplish. Overcome the obstacles and do not stay stagnant. Think about the world as full of colors that illuminate our paradise.

El Amor de Lejos, Entre la Distancia

Veronica Lizardo
Dominican Republic

Mi historia comienza en la ciudad de Santo Domingo, en el barrio Sabana Perdida. Viví en ese barrio diez y nueve años con mi abuela Corina, a quien quiero mucho. Cuando ya yo tenía más conocimiento de la vida, empecé a preguntarme porque nunca viví con mi mamá y mis hermanas menores. Con el tiempo entendí que mi mami tenía bastantes problemas y éramos cinco niñas. Ella tenía que trabajar por nosotras, pero gracias a Dios hoy en día amo y respeto mucho a mami Odalis. Ten en cuenta que solo hay una madre en el mundo y una de esas es la mía.

Con el transcurso de los años me dediqué mucho a mi escuela, El Colegio de La Rosa. Ya para finales de mis estudios en la secundaria, me fui dando cuenta que realmente yo quería para mi futuro—o sea que profesión yo quería estudiar en la universidad. Pero un señor que vive en los Estados Unidos, me vino a buscar para viajar con él—es decir para vivir aquí con él y mis hermanos. Sucedió que para finales de agosto del 2009 ya yo y mis hermanos estábamos aquí. Todo fue tan rápido que no pude terminar mi último año escolar allá en mi país. Hoy en día tengo muchos sueños que realizar, ya que Dios me ha dado la oportunidad de estar en este país para así poder hacer mis estudios más fácilmente.

Pero en esta linda historia de mi vida, también he tenido que pasar por momentos muy difíciles. Cada vez que hablo de este tema, me pongo muy triste. Mis pensamientos se van a esos momentos bellos que viví con esa persona y que jamás olvidaré. Los momentos más lindos que viví fueron con mi novio, con ese chico estuve nueve años hasta que tuve que dejarlo para viajar a New York. Cuando le di la noticia a mi novio, él no le gustó mucho la idea, pero al final lo entendió. Cuando fueron pasando los días, mi novio y yo estábamos muy tristes porque estaba llegando el día de yo irme. No es fácil separarse—al menos para mí—pero uno tiene que ser fuerte para sobrevivir.

El día más triste de mi vida fue el día que estaba en el aeropuerto… Wow. Estuve en un mundo donde la soledad me mataba, creía que el mundo se me venia encima, y no encontraba la forma deshacerme de ese dolor tan grande que sentí al despedirme de las personas que yo más amo.

Hoy en día me siento mucho mejor. Tan solo con saber que mi abuela, mi mamá y mi novio están bien, me siento alegre. Para mí es un privilegio tener la familia que Dios me ha dado. Ellos me valoran mucho. La familia es lo más importante que uno tiene que cuidar porque hoy en día más que nunca hay que tener el apoyo de cada familia.

Digo y expreso todo este sentimiento para que las personas que hayan pasado por este problema tengan la valentía de seguir adelante. No importa si estás lejos o cerca de la persona que tú amas, siempre ten en cuenta el valor de esa persona. Como dice el dicho, "Nadie sabe lo que tiene hasta que lo pierde." Creo que si tenemos esperanza, todo lo que nos proponemos lo podemos lograr. Vence el obstáculo y no te quedes estancado. Piensa en el mundo lleno de colores para iluminar nuestro paraíso.

Thanks to God

Francisco
Dominican Republic

My Childhood

I was born in Santiago, the second largest city in the Dominican Republic, after Santo Domingo. My childhood was good. Thanks to God, I always had my mother's advice. Your only true friends are your mother, your father, and your family.

I had a very difficult experience. One time I got a pain when I was eating. I felt like I was drowning, and then I drank water. It gave me a tachycardia. My heart went "tun tun" so fast, and I told my mom, "Come, already!" My mom got nervous and took me to the hospital. They gave me an injection and it went away.

After some time, a tremendous pain began. I couldn't move, and I felt like I was choking. I spent some time with severe pain. The doctor said that it was an inflation of the layer of the heart. He told me that my heart was expanding because it was growing. I spent about a month going to that doctor, and my mom gave me pills. The pain was so intense that they gave me an injection every 21 days. The injection was so strong that when they gave it to me, I couldn't even walk. My grandmother offered a prayer to God. Thanks to God, it went away.

But it happened again here in New York, as well. I was with my friends and I started to feel ill. I went to the bathroom, I threw the towel that was there on the floor and I lay there. The bathroom was spinning around me, and I heard my friends talking from far away, almost as in a dream. I thought I was going to die. My heart was beating faster than it had in the Dominican Republic. It felt like my heart was coming out of my chest. I kneeled to God and I told him, "God take this from me," and it went away. God is good.

A Blessing from God

I made a mistake recently, but you have to move forward. My girlfriend became pregnant. I say it was a mistake because of my age, but in reality it's a blessing from God. I felt calm because I knew that my mother and my family would support me. I want him to be a good kid. I always hope to be with my son while he's growing up, advise him, and give him a lot of love. I want to study and find a job to be able to give him what he deserves. I also want to always be with my girlfriend. I hope that someday we are husband and wife so that we are together with our baby and the children that are to come, if God gives us health and the strength to succeed in life.

Gracias a Dios

Francisco

Dominican Republic

Mi Niñez

Yo nací en Santiago, la ciudad más grande de la Republica Dominicana después de Santo Domingo. Mi niñez fue buena. Gracias a Dios, siempre tuve el consejo de mi mamá. Me aconseja hasta ahora, hasta que crecí. Los únicos amigos son tu mamá, tu padre y tu familia.

Tuve una experiencia bastante difícil. Una vez me dio un dolor cuando yo estaba comiendo. Me sentía como ahogado y entonces me tragué el agua. Me dio una taquicardia. Mi corazón hacía tun tun rapidísimo y le dije a mami, "Venga ya."

Mi mami se puso nerviosa y me llevó al hospital. Me metieron una inyección y se me quitó.

Después de un tiempo, comenzó un dolor tremendo. Yo no podía moverme y me sentía como asfixiando. Duré un tiempo con un dolor grave. El doctor dijo que era una inflación de la capa del corazón. Me dijo que mi corazón se me estaba como dilatando porque estaba creciendo. Duré como un mes yendo a ese doctor. Mami me daba pastillas. El dolor era tan grande que a mí me ponían una sola inyección cada 21 días. Era tan fuerte la inyección que cuando me ponían eso, yo ni caminar podía. Me abuela le ofreció una oración a Dios. Gracias a Dios se me quitó.

Pero me volvió a pasar aquí en New York también. Estaba con mis amigos y me empecé a sentir mal. Me fui al baño y la toalla que estaba, la tire al suelo y me acosté ahí. El baño se movía a mi alrededor y escuchaba a mis amigos hablando de lejos como entre sueños. Pensaba que me iba a morir. El corazón estaba más rápido que allá—el corazón me salía. Me hinque a Dios y le dije, "Dios quíteme esto." Y se me quitó. Dios es bueno.

Una Bendición de Dios
Yo cometí un error recientemente pero ya hay que echar para delante. La novia mía salió embarazada. Yo digo que fue un error por mi edad pero en realidad es una bendición de Dios. Me sentí tranquilo porque se qué mi mamá y mi familia me van a apoyar.

Yo quiero que ella o él sea un buen muchacho. Yo siempre espero estar con él cuando esté creciendo, aconsejarlo y darle mucho amor. Quiero estudiar y conseguir un trabajo para darle lo que se merece. También quiero estar siempre con mi novia. Espero que algún día seamos marido y mujer para que estemos juntos con nuestro bebé y los niños más que vengan, si Dios nos da la salud y la fuerza para triunfar en la vida.

My Life in the Dominican Republic and New York

Jose Gabriel Muñoz
Dominican Republic

My name is Jose Gabriel Muñoz, but people call me Gabi. I've lived a lot of good times, but some bad ones, too. My childhood was a good time in my life. I liked to go to school and have fun with my friends. I wasn't involved in bad things. I was always having fun with my friends, playing baseball. We used to go to the beach and the dance clubs in Santiago, in my country, the Dominican Republic. A great memory that has always made me very happy is when I won an award for being one of the best pitchers in a competition.

When I was older, I got an appointment at the consulate to get a visa to travel to New York. My father had arranged it for me, and the consulate gave me a visa to travel. I then left for the United States and arrived here on March 19th, 2009. I was very sad to leave my mother, because this is the first time that I've lived with my father. I've missed my mom and my family in Santo Domingo. But when I lived in the Dominican Republic, I always wanted to visit New York, and now I've been able to with the help of my father. Here, I met my six brothers and sisters, and my father enrolled me in the GED Plus Program to finish my diploma so that later I can go to college. Little by little, I'm adapting to this new life in New York. I have also started working.

In the Dominican Republic, I was working at a tourism agency. I was working as a contractor, but they had me doing a lot of different things, and later I became a boat captain. On a dark and rainy day, one time, we had to work, despite the bad weather; the ocean was churning. We had to work on a small island, and so we left for the island on one of the boats. There were lots of big waves and strong winds. We had to travel twelve kilometers. The waves were really bad. I was scared because I thought the boat was going to tip over or sink, and I thought we were all going to drown. When we got to the island, we unloaded all the excursion equipment for the tourists. Just after we landed, they called us to tell us to come back to the mainland because the excursion had been canceled. I felt lost. I thought we were all going to drown, but thank God, we arrived safely to the mainland.

I want to share my story with kids, or give them some good advice, so that they can get ahead in life. When you're young, you have to go through a lot of tough times, and it's good to be able to have something in life that you can call your own.

Mi Vida en Republica Dominicana y New York

José Gabriel Muñoz
Dominican Republic

Mi nombre es José Gabriel Muñoz pero me dicen Gabi. Yo he vivido momentos buenos y a veces momentos malos. Un momento bueno de mi vida fue cuando yo estaba pequeño. Me gustaba siempre ir a la escuela y disfrutar con mis amigos. Nunca he estado en cosas malas. Siempre he estado gozando juntos con todos mis amigos, jugando pelota. Nos íbamos a dar vueltas por la playa, nos íbamos a la disco en mi país, la Republica Dominicana, en la región de Santiago. Un momento bueno que me hizo sentir feliz en mi vida fue cuando me gané un reconocimiento como uno de lo mejores pitcher de un torneo.

Luego después me llegó cita del consulado para viajar a New York. Mi padre me pidió y me dieron la visa para viajar. Después me fui a los Estados Unidos.

Llegué en el 19 de marzo del año 2009. Me sentí muy triste al verme alejado de mi madre, porque era la primera vez que estuviera junto a mi padre. He extrañado a mi madre y a mi familia en Santo Domingo. Siempre en mi país tenia el deseo de conocer a New York hasta que lo pude lograr con la ayuda de mi padre. Aquí llegue a conocer a mis 6 hermano/as. Mi padre me inscribió en el programa de GED Plus para terminar mi diploma para luego ir a la universidad. Poco a poco me estoy adaptando a la nueva vida en New York. Luego comencé a trabajar.

En la Republica Dominicana, estaba trabajando en un compañía de turismo. Yo trabajaba como un contratista. Luego trabajé varios trabajos diferentes pero ellos me asentaron como capitán de bote. En un día muy oscuro y lluvioso teníamos que trabajar con un mal tiempo cuando el mar estaba muy revolteado. Tuvimos que trabajar en la isla y salimos así la isla en uno de lo botes. Había muchos oleajes y vientos muy fuertes. Íbamos a una distancia de 12 kilómetros. Estaba muy mal el oleaje del mar. Yo estaba muy asustado pensando que el bote se iba a voltear o hundirse y pensando que nos íbamos a ahogar. Cuando llegamos a la isla, apeamos todos lo de la excursión para atender los turistas. Poco después que llegamos, llamaron que regresáramos a tierra por que habían cancelado la excursión. En realidad me sentía perdido, pensando que nos íbamos a ahogar todos pero gracias a Dios, llegamos muy bien del viaje de la isla.

Quiero compartir mi historia con toda la juventud, o darle un buen consejo para que puedan salir así adelante. Es que cuando uno esta pequeño, pasa mucho trabajo y es muy bueno tener algo en la vida para decir, "Esto es mío," porque para uno tener algo, tienes que pasar muchas cosas en la vida.

Life's Injustice

Trujillo
Dominican Republic

I was born in Santo Domingo in 1990, where I lived a happy life, going to rivers, beaches, fields, and cities. When we'd go out to the country in Barahona, we'd ride on horseback across the entire town and later go swimming in the river or dancing at nightclubs. Throughout my vacations, I visited many towns and beaches in the south.

Towards the end of one of my summer vacations, I decided to join the local civilian army. I saw all kinds of horrors: deaths, natural disasters, and overall destruction. In my journey from Jimani to Barahona, a man was run over. A train carrying salt from the salt mines hit a bus and the driver was bleeding all over. I went from seeing dead bodies to seeing people injured. If you don't seek help in this sort of situation, you go crazy. You don't know what to do.

When I got back to the city, I was a bit traumatized over what I had seen. It was too much for me at my young age; I was only twelve. I couldn't eat any meat for over two weeks because I couldn't help thinking of the rotting corpses. The first time that I saw so many people dead, I had nightmares and strange dreams for over a month. My mom had to take me to a psychiatrist. He said that I had to go away for a while and relax. So my mom took me to a house in the countryside in a place called Romana where I stayed for a few days. I went to the beach and met some girls. We had lots of fun; I felt that my life was back to normal.

But even so, sometimes I think about what I lived through. Sometimes I think, "Man is nothing." When you see so many dead people, you think, "We are nothing. We are nothing without God." Those people who were once happy are now… I think I had to see those things in order to reflect about my own life and think about the things I shouldn't do. I was one of those carefree boys who didn't care about anything. But something unexpected happened to me. You can't say, "That will never happen to me," because you never know what God has in store for you.

When I Arrived

I came here with my dad, my mom, and my brother. When I came here, I saw a different sort of life—I saw progress. I started studying and working and thinking about my future. I want to pursue many careers. I want to be a doctor or a police officer. I lived on the other side of the law, and now I want to change my life.

It's going to be one year that I've lived in New York. But my thoughts sometimes return to what happened to me when I was little. People ask me, "What happened to you?" I thought the wrong sort of thoughts and did things I shouldn't have done. I even thought about killing myself once… Something that has always helped distract me from bad thoughts is talking to girls. When my mind starts to wander, I do exciting things to bring myself back.

La Injusticia de la Vida

Trujillo
Dominican Republic

Nací en Santo Domingo en 1990 donde viví una vida contenta porque siempre visitabas ríos, playas, campos y ciudades. Cuando íbamos a los campos de Barahona, corríamos en caballos por todo el pueblo, y nos gustaba ir a los ríos y a la discoteca. En el transcurso de mis vacaciones, visité varios pueblos y playas del sur.

Antes de que se terminaran las vacaciones, yo decidí pertenecer a la defensa civil. Tuve que ver diferentes tipos de catástrofes como muertes, desastre, y destrucción. Al transcurso de Jimani para Barahona, atropellaron a un señor en la vía. Un tren que carga yeso de la mina de sal allí en Cabral, le dio a una guagua y el chofer estaba todo desbaratado, herido por donde quiera. Salí de donde habían muertos para pasar donde habían heridos…fue un tiempo muy traumático. Si no tomas ayuda, tú te quieres como volver loco. No sabes que hacer.

Al regresar a la ciudad, yo estaba un poco traumatizado por lo que había visto. Eran demasiadas cosas malas para mi edad—solamente tenía 12 años. Yo duré más o menos como 2 semanas sin comer carne por haber visto esa gente en estado de pudrición. Es trágico. La primera vez que vi tanta gente muerta, tuve más que un mes con pesadillas, sueños raros. Mi mamá tuvo que llevarme donde el psiquiatra cuando estaba en la capital para aliviar el trauma. El siquiatra le dijo que yo tenía que tener unas vacaciones relajadas, sin problemas. Ella me llevó para una casa de campo en la Romana y tuve ahí uno cuantos días relajado. Fui a la playa, conocí varias chicas allá y me divertí mucho. Allá estaba viviendo una vida como normal.

Pero igual pienso hoy en día en eso. A veces tu dices "El hombre no es nadie." Al ver toda esa gente muerta, tu dices, "Nosotros no somos nadie. Sin Dios, nosotros no somos nadie." En un momento, esa gente estaba feliz, contenta, y ahora están… Es algo me hizo reflexionar porque hay veces que uno no piensa y hace cosas que no debes hacer. Yo era un muchacho que siempre vivía como libre, que no le importaba nada. Me pasó algo inesperado. Uno nunca puede decir, "De esta agua no voy a beber" porque uno no sabe lo que Dios le tiene preparado.

Cuando Llegué
Yo vine acá con mi papá, mi mamá, y mi hermano. Cuando vine para acá, vi una vida diferente—progreso. Me puse a estudiar y a trabajar y pensé en mi futuro. Yo quiero estudiar varias carreras. Yo quiero ser médico como también quiero ser policía. Como ya yo viví en una vida que trágica para la policía, vi el lado oscuro de la policía, y ahora quiero cambiar mi vida.

Ya casi voy a cumplir un año aquí en Nueva York. Pero el pensamiento todavía no lo he perdido porque cada vez me acuerdo de eso. Algunas personas, como mi familia, me preguntan ¿Qué fue lo que te pasó? Antes yo pensaba hasta suicidarme, pensaba en cosas que no tenía que pensar, y hacía cosas que no tenía que hacer. Algo que me entretenía a mí para no pensar cosas malas y esas cosas era hablar con las mujeres. A veces me recuerdo de eso y para evitarlo, me pongo a hacer loqueras.

Don't Hold Back On Happiness

Anabel Peralta
Dominican Republic

Nearly everyone calls me 'Susy,' the nickname that my grandmother, Nereida, gave me. I lived with her ever since I was born until about six months ago, when she passed away. Then, I moved to the United States. It's not easy for me to get used to the idea that she's gone after living with her for 18 happy years. But I feel better when I remember that I respected her and treated her well. I want to tell you about what she was like and give you some very important advice—advice that might be useful one day when someone you love passes away.

Even though she was 68 years old, my grandmother was full of life and happiness. She was someone who liked to smile and make others smile. What my grandma liked to do the most was to be around her family and see new places and things. She was someone who cared about the well-being of those around her. She was a hard-working woman and, when she died, left an emptiness in our family and in all those who knew her.

I remember the night she died—August 14th. That day was no different from any other. She looked fine and didn't mention feeling sick. She decided to visit her mother (my great-grandmother Graciela). Even though she went there every Sunday, she went on a Friday instead. When we got to my great-grandmother's house, my great-grandmother was feeling a bit dizzy and told my grandmother, "Any day now, I'm going to die from one of these ailments." My grandmother answered, "You like to say silly things, don't you? Watch me go before you do." My great-grandmother told us to come back on Sunday because she was planning to cook for all of us…

My grandmother went home, watched some TV, and then we headed to her son, my uncle, Miguelito's house. My grandmother, my grandfather Teofilo, my cousins Anxony and Alex, my older sister Mabel, and I all lived together. We had so much fun talking at my uncle's house until about seven pm, when we all headed back home. My grandmother sat back down in front of the TV, and then took a bath. When she was done she told us—my cousins Miyorquis, Mayerlys, and I—that we could keep watching TV, because it was still early. She went to bed at five past eleven. I heard my grandfather yelling that something was going on. When I went to look, she was already gone.

I don't know how to explain how I felt. It was the worst thing I had ever lived through. I didn't know what I was doing—I just kept talking to her to see if she'd answer me. I ran barefoot all the way to my uncle Miguelito's house, not realizing that I had already called him on the phone. My neighbors heard me screaming and came over. I didn't want to hear anyone confirm that she was dead, because I couldn't believe it, even after having seen her.

They took her to a clinic. I kept calling my aunt Yorquiris, who kept saying that my grandmother was fine, just to keep me calm. I asked her to put my grandmother on the phone to see if she'd wake up if she heard my voice, but my aunt wouldn't do it. When they brought my grandmother back to the house at two-thirty, I didn't have the courage to look at her because I was still in shock.

I kept asking myself why God hadn't taken me instead. Then I understood that this happened because God willed it. He knows what's best, but even so, I still felt bad and couldn't see her until five in the morning. Every day that goes by since her funeral, the pain gets worse and worse. People keep telling me to give it time, but time hasn't healed anything. I miss her more and more, and it hurts that she's gone.

Twenty-five days after my grandmother died, I moved to the United States. Things aren't the same after you lose someone, especially if you lose someone you loved as much as I loved my grandmother. Your life just isn't the same; you don't have the same desire to live. Everything seems flat; even when something happens that should hurt you, you don't feel the pain because it doesn't compare with your suffering. Through this pain, though, you finally discover your soul.

I have learned that love for our parents is the root of our humanity. It teaches us where we come from and who we are, and it leads us to where we're going and what we want and hope for in life. Treat your parents well and respect them, because respect gives peace and serenity. Don't hold back on happiness, because happiness doesn't hurt anyone. Give them love because love is the most valuable thing in life, and you'll have a great, happy family. If you do this, I am sure that when the day comes when you lose someone, you won't feel bad because you will have given them all you could while they were with you. I say this because I lived through it myself.

No Se Limite en Darle Felicidad

Anabel Peralta
Dominican Republic

Casi todos me llaman Susy, el apodo que me dio mi abuela Nereida. Desde que nací, siempre viví con ella hasta hace seis meses que se murió. Entonces tuve que venir para los Estados Unidos. No es fácil para mi acostumbrarme a la idea que ya no esta después de vivir casi 18 años con ella llenos de felicidad. Pero me siento mejor porque sé que la traté bien y la respeté. Por esta razón quiero contarle sobre como era ella y darle un consejo muy importante. Un consejo que si lo siguen, le va hacer útil para si algún día le llega a faltar alguien importante, sea sus padres u otra persona a la que quieran.

A pesar de tener 68 años de edad, mi mamá era una persona llena de vida y alegría. Era una persona que le gustaba sonreír y hacer sonreír a los demás y hacerlos feliz. Lo que más le gustaba a mi mamá era estar en familia y pasear y conocer cosas nuevas. Era una mujer luchadora y al irse, no solo nos dejó un gran vacío a nuestra familia, si no a todos lo que la conocían.

Si preguntan como murió, fue la noche del 14 de agosto. Ese día era uno como cualquier otro. Ella se veía bien y no nos dijo que se sentía mal. Ese día decidió ir para donde su mamá Graciela, donde ella siempre iba todas los domingos. Pero en esa semana, decidió ir ese viernes. Cuando llegamos a la casa de su mamá, su mamá estaba mala y se sentía un poco mareada y como cosas de gente mayor le dijo a mi abuela, "Yo creo que ya yo me voy a morir de tantas cosas." Después mi abuela le respondió, "A usted si le gusta decir cosas. Cuando viene a ver yo me muero primero que usted." Ese día Graciela dijo que el domingo volviera, que ella iba a cocinar para todos...

Después de llegar a la casa ella vio televisión y luego fue para donde su hijo Miguelito y mi tia Yorquiris. Mi abuela, mi abuelo Teofilo, mis primos Alex y Anxony, mi hermana mayor, Mabel, y yo vivíamos todos juntos. Pasamos un gran rato allá hablando y luego como a las 7 de la noche se fue para su casa y se puso a ver televisión otra vez. Luego se fue a bañar y cuando terminó nos dijo a mis primás Miyorquis, Mayerlys y a mí que podíamos seguir viendo televisión porque todavía era temprano. Entonces se acostó como a las 11:05 PM y luego mi abuelo me llamó que le estaba pasando algo. Cuando fui a ver la ya estaba muerta.

No sé como explicar lo que sentí. Es lo peor que me había pasado en mi vida. No supe lo que hice, solo le hablaba para ver si me respondía y después salí para afuera a buscar a mi tío Miguelito para su casa. Salí descalza y no me di cuenta que ya lo había llamado por teléfono y toda las gente que vivían cerca al oírme gritando fueron para la casa. No quería oír a nadie que dijera que si estaba muerta porque aun yo viéndola muerta no lo podía creer.

Luego se la llevaron para la clínica bien rápido. No dejé ni un minuto de llamar para ver si respondía y mi tía Yorquiris me decía que sí que estaba bien pero solo me lo decía para que me calmara. Le pedía que le pusiera el teléfono en sus oídos para hablarle para ver si despertaba pero no quiso. Luego cuando la llevaron para la casa como a las 2:30 AM no tenía el valor de ir y verla en la cara porque no lo podía creerlo.

Me preguntaba que porque no me paso a mí y no a ella. Pero luego entendí que si paso, es por que Dios lo permitió y El sabe qué nos conviene pero aun así me seguía sintiendo mal y no fui capaz de verla hasta como las cinco de la mañana. Después de su entierro el dolor era más grande y cada día que pasa es más grande. Algunas personas dicen que con el tiempo duele menos pero eso no esta pasando conmigo. Cada día la extraño más y me duele más que ya no esta.

Después de pasar veinticinco días que mi mamá murió tuve que venir para los Estados Unidos. Ya no es lo mismo cuando pierdes a alguien, más si lo quieres tanto como yo quería a mi abuela. Tu vida ya no es la misma—ya no tienes los mismos deseos de vivir. Todo te da igual, sientes un gran dolor que cuando te pasa algo que te puede doler ni lo sientes porque es más grande el dolor que tienes. Si no sabías lo que es el alma lo descubres, pero la gran pena es que la descubres con un gran dolor.

Y aprendí que el amor a nuestros padres es la base de todo ser humano porque nos enseña de donde venimos y quienes somos y nos da las pautas para saber hacia donde vamos y que queremos y esperamos de la vida. Trate a sus padres bien y respételos porque el respeto es paz y tranquilidad. No se limite en darle felicidad porque la felicidad no hiere. Déle todo el amor que pueda porque el amor es lo más lindo y valioso que hay en la vida y así serán una gran familia llena de felicidad. Si hace esto que le digo sé que si algún día le llega a faltar unos de sus padres, no se sentirá tan mal porque van a saber que le dio lo más importante que necesitaban mientras estaban con Usted. Le digo todo esto porque ya lo viví.

My Story and My Family's Story

Pimentel

Dominican Republic

My name is Pimentel, and I am 19 years old. My father came here, to the United States, last Saturday, and I am happy because, now, my family is together. My family is with me, and they are going to be with me for my birthday, which is March 15th. I am happy that they we will all be together. Thank God!

My life in the Dominican Republic was good, because I always had my father and my mother by my side. I never strayed away from them or from my brother, either, in good times and bad times. I lived a very good life in Santo Domingo, and I was happy there. I would go out, enjoy myself, go to parties, and be with my friends—chill with them. I was always the type of person who liked to enjoy myself and have fun. I never liked to be sad, but there are some days in life that you become sad because of the things that happen in your family and to people you love.

Well, when we got here, we went through a lot because we lived with my grandmother and she lived in an old folks' home. So, my little brother and I had to be sent to Santo Domingo for six months because we didn't have a place to live here. In Santo Domingo, I worked to buy another plane ticket to come back here.

When I came back, there were six of us that lived in one room. It wasn't too big of a room; half of us slept on the floor and the other half slept on a bed that was there. We went through a lot because we went hungry, very hungry. You see me a little chubby now, but I wasn't like this when I lived in that room. When I got here, it was the first time that I actually starved. When I lived with my father in Santo Domingo, he did whatever he could to feed us. Even if he didn't have a job, he would say, "Let me do this little job to feed my children." But when I got here, from one moment to the next, I didn't think I would starve. And it is very hard to go without food; I don't wish it on my worst enemy. I got very skinny and my nephew who was very little got worse—skinny, very skinny. We had to do whatever was possible to find a home, because my nephew didn't look too good; now, he is a little fatter. We didn't eat for a while. My brother, the older one who worked, would only bring food sometimes because they didn't pay him a lot of money. My mother brought us food on the weekends. But it was not everyday that we ate.

We spent about six months in that one room, and then we moved to a house in Westchester. We were fine there, but we were living without heat because the heating system wasn't very good. We had to buy a space heater to warm up the house. Now, I am living with an aunt of mine. She treats me well, and I love her just as she loves me. I live with her just fine, and I don't have to go through any hardships because she gives me everything I need.

In school, everyone always asks me why I am so happy, and they tell me that I am very, very open. But, Ms. Jackie sometimes tells me that I look as if I were sad. Ms. Jackie asks me, "That face isn't yours, what's the matter?" She always asks me that, and I tell her, "No, Ms. Jackie, I am fine, it's just that I have to be calm some days." And Ms. Jackie responds, "No, I like to see you smile, because you look happier when you're smiling." And I say, "Oh, well you're going to see me laugh everyday." But here, in school, all of my peers tell me that I am a happy person and in my household, too. To me, my mother is everything because when she sees me happy, she is happy, and so I start telling her things so that she will laugh. Everyone tells me that I am a very happy person.

I feel good in the US, because I am adapting to life here. For example, I have made friends; I'm living well, and I am studying to reach my career goal. I feel that I have progressed a lot in the United States. I intend to have a career that I like; I would like to be a civil engineer.

Mi Historia y la de Mi Familia

Pimentel
Dominican Republic

Me llamo Marlene Pimentel y tengo 19 años. Mi padre llego aquí, a los Estados Unidos, el Sábado pasado y estoy alegre porque ahora, la familia mía esta junta. Mi familia esta conmigo y van a estar conmigo en mi cumpleaños que es el 15 de marzo. Estoy alegre de que estén conmigo gracias a Dios.

En la Republica Dominicana, yo viví con mis padres muy bien. Mi vida en la Republica Dominicana era bien porque yo vivía con mi papá y mi mamá, y nunca me separé de ellos, ni de mi hermano tampoco. Yo quiero mucho a mi familia porque son muy unidos y siempre están en la buena y en la mala. Yo vivía muy bien en Santo Domingo y era feliz allá. Yo andaba, gozaba, iba a las fiestas, estaba con mis amigos, jangueaba con ellos. Siempre me ha gustado ser divertida y alegre. A mí nunca me ha gustado estar triste pero hay algunos días en tu vida que uno se pone triste por cosas que pasan de tu familia y de personas que tu quieres.

Bueno, cuando nosotros llegamos aquí, pasamos mucho porque yo vivía con una abuela mía y la abuela mía vivía en un apartamento que era para viejitos. Entonces al mas chiquito de mis hermanos y a mí, nos tuvieron que mandar a Santo Domingo durante seis meses porque no teníamos adonde vivir aquí. En Santo Domingo, trabajé para volver a comprar mi vuelo para volver para atrás.

Cuando volví para atrás, éramos seis personas que vivíamos en un solo cuarto. No era tan grande -- una mitad dormía en el piso y la otra en una cama que había. Nosotros pasamos mucho, porque pasamos hambre, mucha hambre. Tú me ves así gordita pero yo no estaba así cuando yo vivía en esa habitación. Cuando yo llegué aquí fue la primera vez que pase hambre. Cuando yo vivía con mi papá en Santo Domingo, él hacia todo lo posible para darnos comida. El, aunque no tuviera trabajando, decía "Ven que yo hago este trabajito para darle comida a mis hijos." Pero de un momento a otro, cuando yo llegué aquí, yo no pensé que yo iba pasar hambre. Y es duro pasar hambre y no se lo deseo ni a mi peor enemigo. Yo me puse flaquita y mi sobrinito que era chiquitito se puso peor, flaquito flaquito. Nosotros tuvimos que hacer lo posible por conseguir una casa porque mi sobrinito estaba feo y ahora es que esta mas gordito. Nosotros no comíamos. Mi hermano, el grande que trabajaba, llevaba comida a veces porque no le pagaban mucho. Mi mamá nos traía comida en los fines de semana. Pero no todos los días nosotros comíamos.

Después duramos como seis meses ahí en esa habitación y después nos mudamos para una casa ahí en Westchester. Y ahí estábamos bien pero estábamos pasando frío también porque la calefacción no era muy fuerte en esa casa. Estuvimos que comprar un heater para que la casa se caliente. Ahora mismo yo estoy viviendo con una tía mía. Ella me trata muy bien y yo la quiero mucho a ella y ella me quiere mucho a mí. Yo vivo con ella muy bien y no tengo que pasar nada porque ella me da todo lo que yo necesito y cosas así.

Siempre aquí en la escuela todo el mundo me dice que porque yo soy tan alegre y que yo soy muy, muy abierta. Ms. Jackie me dice a veces que yo vengo con la cara como que estoy triste. Ms. Jackie me dice, "Y esa cara no es la tuya, que tu tienes?" Siempre me pregunta eso y yo le digo, "No Ms. Jackie, yo estoy tranquila, lo que pasa es que hay que estarse tranquila en un día." Y Ms. Jackie dice, "No, a mí me gusta verte sonreír porque tú te ves más, más alegre así sonriéndote." Y yo, "A pues me va ver todo los días riéndome." Pero aquí en la escuela todos los muchachos me dicen que yo soy alegre y en mi casa también. Mi mamá conmigo es de todo porque cuando me ve alegre, ella está alegre y yo comienzo a decirle cosas para que ella se ria también. Todo el mundo me dice que yo soy muy alegre.

En los Estados Unidos, yo me siento bien porque me estoy acostumbrando a estar aquí. Por ejemplo, he encontrado amigos, yo me la estoy pasando muy bien y yo estoy estudiando para llegar hacer mi profesión. Yo siento que yo he progresado mucho en los Estados Unidos. Yo tengo un propósito para obtener una carrera que me gusta. Me gustaría ser ingeniera en civil.

Alejandro, the Blessing of My Life

Leticia

Honduras

When I became pregnant with Alejandro, I was 17 years old. I had him when I was 18 years old, when I was finishing my last year in high school. I graduated when I was two months pregnant, but I didn't know I was pregnant until the third month when I went to the doctor.

I had a lot of problems with Alejandro's father because he wanted me to have an abortion, and I didn't want one. I wanted to have my baby. He was the man whom I wanted to be with. I wanted to have a family with him, but when I gave him the news that I was pregnant, he got very angry. He didn't want me to have the baby. When he told me that, he broke my heart, because he knew that I wanted to have my baby. He made me choose between him and the baby.

I told my mother that I was pregnant and she told me to think about what I really wanted. I decided to have my baby without caring about what others thought of me, without caring about whether or not his father supported me. I had my mother by my side, the person who supported me through good times and bad times. My mother helped during my pregnancy, because Alejandro's father only gave me three apples throughout the nine months. My mother came with me to my appointments and took me everywhere, because my pregnancy was high risk. I couldn't even bend down to put my shoes on, or put on my shirt, nothing. My mother did everything. I couldn't even sleep. I could only sit or lie down with my feet toward the wall.

When I went to the doctor, I was told that my baby was having heart complications. When I received that news, it shattered my heart because I only thought about the fact that my small baby could die or that he was suffering. I got very sad. I decided to call my son's father to see what he would tell me. And he told me, "It is your fault, because you don't feed him well." And I told him, "But if you don't give me money, how do you want me to feed him?" He replied, "That's why you have your mother, so that you can be fed." After that, I didn't ask for anything else, because my mother gave me everything.

One Sunday, my water broke. I didn't have pain, and I was with my mother at the laundromat. At eight in the evening, I told my mother and she took me to the hospital. My blood was taken and they hooked me up to an IV. After that, I fell asleep, but when I awoke in the morning, I had a lot of back pain. I felt like my back was broken. I could not lie down; it was very painful. My baby wanted to come out, but I was not dilating enough for him to do so. They gave me some treatment, so that I would dilate more.

At four in the afternoon, the pain became greater and the contractions were stronger. I was becoming impatient, and I asked the doctor to give me the epidural. The pain was so great that I couldn't even feel it when they gave me the injection. Afterward, I couldn't feel the pain anymore. At five forty-five in the afternoon, you could see my baby's head. I felt happy when my baby was finally born. I looked at him and in that moment, I was the happiest person in the world because I had a beautiful and healthy child. My mother cut the umbilical cord. They put him on my chest and cleaned him. He moved a lot and was very fat. I was very nervous, but happy at the same time. He slept like an angel in my arms. When I looked at him, I thanked God for giving him to me healthy and very strong.

As Alejandro grew, he laughed with me. He knew my voice when I read to him and he laughed. I played with him and tickled him on the stomach. At four months, Alejandro started to crawl, and at eight months, he began to walk. He touched everything and laughed at everything. He is now one year old and is a precious and playful baby. He adores my mother and my brothers, and he also plays with Osita and me.

He has taught me that the most beautiful thing is to love and to be loved, because I love my baby and I know that he loves me. Alejandro is everything to me. He is the motor of my life. Your mother loves you, Alejandro.

La Bendición De Mi Vida Es Alejandro

Leticia

Honduras

Cuando yo salí embarazada de Alejandro tenía 17 años. Lo tuve a los 18 años, cuando estaba sacando mi octavo grado. Yo me gradué cuando yo tenía dos meses de embarazo porque yo salí embarazada pero yo no me di cuenta hasta que yo tenía tres meses y fui para el doctor.

Tuve muchos problemas con el papá de Alejandro porque él quería que yo abortara y yo no quería. Yo quería tener mi bebé. El fue el hombre con quien quería estar. Deseaba tener una familia con él pero cuando yo le di la noticia que yo estaba embarazada, se enojo mucho. No quería que yo tuviera mi bebé. Cuando él me dijo eso, me rompió el corazón por que él sabía que yo deseaba tener mi bebé. Él me puso a elegir entre mi bebé o él.

Yo le comenté a mi mamá que estaba embarazada y ella me dijo que pensara lo que realmente quería. Decidí tener a mi bebé sin importarme lo que pensaran de mi, sin importarme si el papá me apoyara. Tenía mi madre a mi lado, una persona que me apoyó en las buenas y en las malas. Mi mamá me ayudó con el embarazo porque el papá de Alejandro solamente me dió tres manzanas durante los nuevos meses. Mi mamá iba conmigo a la citas y me llevaba para todos lados, porque mi embarazo fue de alto riesgo. Yo no podía ni agacharme a ponerme los zapatos, ni podía ponerme mi camisa, nada. Todo me lo hacía mi mamá. No podía ni barrer. Solo estaba sentaba o acostada con los pies para la pared.

Cuando yo fui para el doctor, me dijeron que mi bebé estaba enfermo del corazón. Cuando yo recibí esa noticia me destrozaron el corazón de solo pensar que mi pequeño bebé se me podía morir o que estaba sufriendo. Me ponía muy triste. Decidí llamar al papá de mi hijo para ver que me decía. Y él me dijo, "Es tu culpa porque tu no te alimentas bien". Y yo le dije a él, "¿Pero si tú no me das dinero como quieres que me alimente?" "Para eso tú tienes a tu mamá para que tú te alimentes." Entonces yo no le pedí nada más, porque mi mamá me daba todo.

Un domingo a mí se me rompió la fuente; no me dieron dolores y yo estaba con mi mamá en el laundry. A las 8 de la noche, yo le comenté a mi mamá y me llevó para al hospital. Me sacaron sangre y me pusieron suero. Después de eso, me quede dormida, pero cuando me levanté en la mañana tenía mucho dolor en la espalda. Sentía que se me partía. No podía estar acostada—era un dolor muy fuerte. Mi bebé ya quería nacer pero yo no abría lo suficiente para que naciera. Me pusieron un tratamiento para que pudiera abrir.

Cuando eran las 4 de la tarde, el dolor se hacía más grade y las contracciones eran más fuertes. Me estaba desesperando y le pedí al doctor que me pusiera la epidural. Era tanto el dolor que no sentí nada cuando me la pusieron. Después no sentí más dolor. A las 5:45 mi bebé ya se le veía la cabeza. Me puse muy feliz cuando por fin mi bebé pudo nacer. Lo mire y en ese momento era la mujer más feliz del mundo por que tenía a un bebé hermoso y saludable. Mi mamá le corto el ombligo. Lo pusieron en mi pecho y lo limpiaron. Se movía mucho y era muy gordo. Estaba muy nerviosa y al mismo tiempo feliz. Se quedaba como un angelito dormido entre mis brazos. Cuando lo miraba, le daba gracias a Dios por dármelo sano y muy fuerte.

A medida que Alejandro iba creciendo, se reía conmigo. Conocía mi voz cuando yo le leía y el se reía. Yo jugaba con él y le hacía cosquillitas en la barriga. A los cuatro meses Alejandro empezó a gatear y a los ocho meses empezó a caminar. Tocaba todo y se reía de todo. Ahora tiene un año y es un bebé precioso y juguetón. Adora a mi mamá y a mis hermanos y también juega con Osita y conmigo.

Me ha enseñado que lo más bello es amar y ser amado porque yo amo a mi bebé y yo sé que él me ama a mí. Alejandro es todo para mí. Es el motor de mi vida. Mamá te ama, Alejandro.

Has Destiny Ever Changed Your Beliefs?

Lisael Ovalle
Dominican Republic

My Beautiful Childhood
My childhood was very peaceful. I was born in a village called Arroyo Caña in Santo Domingo. Arroyo Caña is a very happy village where the people are very kind and love me dearly. I was raised with my grandparents, and they gave me the support that I needed when I was in primary school. It took me nine years to finish primary school because I had to repeat the seventh grade, since I didn't pay attention in class. I was always fooling around with my friends and joking with them, but thanks to my grandfather and God, I finished. Then I went to high school, but I couldn't finish my first year because I came to the United States. Throughout my childhood in Arroyo Caña, my grandparents gave me the upbringing I needed to become the person I am today. I want everyone who reads my story to be aware of the fact that your upbringing is important and also that care and respect bring peace.

My Friends and I
With what I learned from my childhood, I helped my friends a lot. The same things I learned, I was able to teach the people close to me. My friends were always important to me, because we were always telling jokes. But I would explain to them how they should act around their parents. If they behaved, everything would be fine; but if they didn't, everything would take a turn for the worse. I learned this from my uncle, who always reprimanded me for the bad things I did. If I misbehaved, he would scold me, but he always gave me advice

so that I wouldn't get into trouble with other people. I never had problems with anybody because of his advice. I am thankful to have him because he always made sure that I had everything so that I wouldn't encounter problems with the other boys.

My Advice

I gave that same advice to my nephew, so that he'd have a great role model to follow and so that he grows with the best education possible—so that when he gets older, he can share the advice with others or give even better advice. Also, so that he can give it to more children so that they have the knowledge and respect each other. He never followed my advice, though, and was always a pain with my grandparents and his mother. He would sneak away and walk around because he always wanted to be around me. He'd follow me because I was the one who bought him his milk, ice cream, and crackers. For this reason, he liked me more than his mother. But I always told him that he couldn't follow me around because the guys that I hung out with were older than me and he was only two years old. But either way, I loved him because he was my first nephew. I miss him a lot, I miss all my friends, and especially my grandfather. I want to tell them that even though I am far away, I will never forget them, because I love them all. I learned that the most important thing in life is to never forget your past or your family, no matter where you are.

¿El Destino Alguna Vez Le Ha Cambiado Sus Ilusiones?

Lisael Ovalle
Dominican Republic

Mi Linda Niñez
Mi niñez fue una niñez muy sana. Yo nací y me crié en un campo llamado Arroyo Caña en Santo Domingo. Arroyo Caña es un campo muy alegre y donde la gente era muy buena y me querían mucho. Yo me crié con mis abuelos y ellos me daban el apoyo que yo necesitaba cuando entre a la escuela primaria. Me duró 9 años para poder terminar la primaria porque perdí el 7 grado porque no le ponía atención a la clase. Yo siempre estaba jugando con mis amigos y estaba siempre en chiste, pero gracias a mi abuelo y a Dios, la terminé. Luego fui a la high school pero no pude terminar mi primer grado porque vine a los Estados Unidos. Durante mi niñez en Arroyo Caña, mis abuelos me dieron la crianza que yo necesitaba para poder ser quien soy hoy día. Yo quiero que todos los que lean esta historia se den cuenta que la crianza vale mucho y que el cariño y el respeto es la paz. También que si le dan el apoyo que su hijo necesita, sea bueno, siempre se lo va agradecer.

Mis Amigos y Yo
Después de todo esto yo ayudé mucho a mis amigos porque esa enseñanza se les puede aplicar a otras personas que sean cercanos a tí. Mis amigos siempre eran muy importante para mí porque siempre vivíamos haciendo chistes. Pero yo le explicaba como ellos tenían que ser con sus padres porque si se portan bien todo le sale bien, pero si se portan mal, todo le va a salir mal. Eso me lo enseñó mi tío, que siempre estaba reclamándome lo malo que yo hacía. Si yo me portaba mal, él me reclamaba mal, pero siempre me dio un buen consejo para que no me metiera en problema con los muchachos de más, y nunca tuve problema con nadie por eso. Yo se lo agradezco a él también porque él buscaba

que yo estuviera lo mejor posible para que no tuviera un problema con los demás muchachos.

Mis Consejos

Ese mismo consejo se lo estaba yo dando a mi sobrino para que tuviera un buen ejemplo, para que se criara con la mejor educación posible. Para que cuando él tenga el tamaño, él pueda dar el ejemplo que yo le di o un ejemplo mejor que el que yo le enseñe. También para que él pueda aplicárselo a los demás niños para que los otros niños tengan educación y se respeten. Aunque él no se llevaba de esos consejos y siempre estaba de cabezudo con mi abuelos y con su mamá y se le escapaba para irse andar, porque siempre quería estar detrás de mi. Porque yo le compraba leche y le compraba helado y le compraba galletita, por eso él me quería más que a su mamá. Pero yo siempre le decía que no podía andar detrás de mí porque los muchachos con que yo andaba eran mayor que yo y él tenia solo dos años. Pero comoquiera yo lo quería mucho porque era mi primer sobrino.

Eso es lo único que yo espero de el cuando yo valla para Santo Domingo, porque lo extraño mucho a él y a todos mis amigos y a mi abuelo especialmente. Le quiero decir que aunque yo esté lejos, nunca lo voy a olvidar porque lo amo a todos. Yo aprendí que lo más importante en la vida es nunca olvidarse de su pasado y sus familiares, donde quiera que uno esté.

My World Changed Thanks to You

La Negra Rodriguez
Dominican Republic

For those of you who are feeling down, never remain defeated, because at the end of the road, there is always hope. This is my story. My life has been really good because ever since I was little, my parents always gave me everything I wanted, treated me well, and gave me all their love and affection. But everything changed suddenly because they separated.

When I was one year old, my mom went to Panama, and she left me with my dad and my sister. So I stayed with him and with my sister. After that, my mom returned, but after eight years, they separated again, and that's when my father came over here. My dad remarried and he tried to arrange for me to join him in New York, but he wasn't able to make it happen. I was living with my mom and was in very little touch with my dad. The problem was that even though my dad's new wife invited me to live with them, it seemed he wasn't doing anything to make that possible; I needed a passport, and he didn't do anything to get me one.

Even though I always spent time with my mom's family and not my dad's, I always felt closer to my dad than my mom. I always loved him more even though he was far away. He didn't treat me with much love, but little by little he started to change. Even though he started calling us more, the problems continued. The problems had to do with how he was with women and how they were with him. They also had to do with the fact that the only thing that mattered to my dad was moving to this country and earning money.

I also had some problems with my mom, a while back, because I was with a colleague of hers who was a married man. Because of that, I moved out of her house when I was fifteen and went to live with my grandmother on my dad's side. I spent three years living with my grandmother when he and I broke up. I thought he was my life, but it turned out he wasn't. He never did anything for me and it was all for nothing.

Then, God gave me an amazing man, and my world has changed because of him. He helped me in a lot of ways, and my life got much better after we started dating, because I was happier. From the moment I met him, I felt that my heart was full of fear, a hopeful fear. I don't know why that happened, but I think my heart started beating fast because it was inspired by something beautiful. When I looked into his eyes, I saw a man who was pure and sincere.

Around that time I moved to Jarabacoa, another city in the Dominican Republic. My mom didn't want to have anything to do with me after what I had done. We didn't speak for six months. When we started speaking again, I learned that my mom was traveling back and forth to Spain. This was all a surprise, but then she started sending me money in case I needed anything.

My whole life was different, because I was living in the country, which I didn't like, but I got used to living and studying there. I made a big decision in my life. I decided I want to study, get a degree, and one day become a professional. I want to be independent—become a professional, get married, and have my own family. In this country you have to stand on your own two feet, which makes life harder.

When you are new to something, often it seems more difficult. In life there are always challenges to overcome. That's why I try to learn from my mistakes, so I don't hit the same walls. My life is better because I learned that lesson.

Mi Mundo Cambio Gracias A Tí

La Negra Rodriguez
Dominican Republic

Para los que estén tristes, nunca se den por vencido porque al final del camino siempre hay una esperanza. Esta es mi historia. Mi vida ha sido muy buena porque desde chiquita, mis padres siempre me dieron todo lo que yo quería, me trataron bien, pero si me añoñaron un poco. Pero todo cambió de pronto porque ellos se separaron.

Cuando yo tenía un año, mi mamá se fue a Panamá y me dejó con mi papá y mi hermana. Entonces yo me quedé con él y con mi hermana. Después de eso, mi mamá volvió, pero a los ocho años ellos se separaron de nuevo y de ahí fue que mi papá vino para acá. Mi papá se casó y luego me estaba haciendo los papeles para venirme a vivir para acá y no se pudo. En esos momentos, yo estuve con mi mamá y hablaba poco con él. El problema fue que su esposa, con la que él se caso, me pidió pero él parece que no hizo lo posible, o sea no hizo nada, porque me hacia falta el pasaporte y él no hizo lo posible por sacarlo.

Yo siempre estaba con la familia de mi mamá, no con la de mi papá, pero yo siempre estuve más pegada a él que a mi mamá. Siempre lo quise más a él, pero él era más alejado. No me trataba así con tanto amor pero ya poco a poco él fue cambiando. El fue llamando y más cosas pero siempre tuvimos problemas. Los problemas eran resultado de la forma como él tenía las mujeres y como ellas eran con él. También porque lo que le importaba era venir aquí o el dinero que él tenia, no le importaba más nada.

Tuve muchos problemas con mi mamá un tiempo atrás porque yo estuve con un colega de ella pero él tenía a su mujer. Y a eso de los 15 años, yo me separé de ella y fui a vivir con mi abuela, la mamá de mi papá. En ese tiempo, yo duré 3 años allá con mi abuela, pero creía que todo se me iba acabar porque me alejaron de él. Yo creía que era mi vida pero no era así. El nunca hizo nada por mí. Todo fue en vano.

Dios me puso en el camino a un hombre maravilloso y mi mundo cambio por el. El me ayudo en muchas cosas y mi vida después de ahí era más feliz porque me sentía bien. En el momento en que lo vi, sentí que mi corazón tenia miedo. No se porque me paso eso, pero creo que mi corazón latió al verlo a el porque me inspiro algo lindo. Al verlo a el, al ver sus ojos, vi un hombre puro y sincero.

También en ese tiempo que yo me mudé para Jarabacoa, mi mamá ya no quería saber de mí y no me quería ni ver por lo que hice. Duramos más de 6 meses que ni nos hablábamos, después empezamos a hablar y ella estaba haciendo viajes para España pero no lo sabía. Todo fue de sorpresa, pero luego me empezó a mandar dinero para que no me faltara nada.

Todo era diferente porque era en un campo y a mí no me gustaba ir aya. Pero me fui acostumbrando y estaba estudiando. Yo tomé una decisión en mi vida de que yo quiero estudiar y quiero terminar mis estudios y ser una profesional. Yo quiero ser una profesional, quiero tener mi familia, quiero casarme, y no depender de mi familia. Pero en este país tú tienes que salir adelante por tí mismo, no por nadie y ese es el problema.

Cuando tú no tienes muchos conocimientos de algo, muchas veces las cosas se te hacen más difícil. En la vida tienes que pasar por muchos retos, los cuales tienes que superar. Por eso yo he aprendido mucho de mis errores y quiero hacer las cosas bien para no tropezar con la misma piedra.

The Path of Hope

Yomari Salcedo
Dominican Republic

I was born September 5th, 1990, in the province of Monseñol Nouel (Bonao). I moved in with my boyfriend when I was fifteen years old. When I moved in with him, my parents were very worried about me, because I was so young. They went looking for us, but later they decided to leave us alone. I heard them saying that they were going to have my boyfriend (who is now my husband) arrested. Dad went around looking for him, but people advised him to leave us alone. Later, my father asked me if this was what I really wanted. But I could smell my new life in front of me, and its fragrance smelled like hope. I held my husband's hands in my own, and told him that we needed to get ahead in our lives, together, so that we could show everyone that we could make it together in a new place.

After two years, we decided to have a baby. His name is Ordalis Junior G.S. When my son turned two years old, I got the papers that I had been waiting for; I got residency here. I had to leave my son and his father behind to come to the United States. I came to find a better future for all of us. I have suffered a lot, because I had to leave my son and his father. But I'm very proud of my husband, because he has supported our son and me. That's why I need to work very hard to help my family and bring them to this country.

I want my mother to bring my father here. He is the best father in the world. I came to the United States with my mother, because my grandfather (my mother's father), asked us to come. We had to leave my father, my son, and my husband, but when we have the money, we will bring them all, God willing. My husband is a good father, because when my son and I need him most, he's there for us. For example, my son was very sick and was hospitalized for a week, and his father was there by his side the entire time, because I couldn't be. Thank God my son survived, and now he is a healthy and intelligent boy.

I'm working now so that I can afford to visit my family in my country, and when I have the money, I'm going to bring them to the United States. I've been living in the States now for four months, and I like it because it is a developed country. A piece of advice that I'd like to give to all the young girls out there, don't marry young. Wait until the right time comes, and think about it before jumping in too early.

El Camino de la Esperanza

Yomari Salcedo
Dominican Republic

Nací el 5 de septiembre del 1990 en la provincia Monseñor Nouel (Bonao). Me mudé con mi novio a los quince años de edad. Cuando me mudé con mi novio, vi que mis padres estaban preocupados. Ellos nos andaban buscando, pero más tarde pensaron dejarnos tranquilos. Yo escuchaba a ellos decir que iban a meter preso a mi novio, quien ahora es mi esposo. Papi lo andaba buscando pero luego lo aconsejaron y él dijo que nos iba a dejar tranquilos. Luego mi padre habló conmigo y me preguntó si que eso era lo que yo quería. Me dio el olor de una nueva vida por recordar con fragancias de la esperanza. Yo toqué las manos de mi esposo y dijimos que teníamos que echar adelante juntos para poder estar bien juntos en un lugar nuevo.

Después de estar juntos por dos años, decidimos tener un niño. Su nombre es Ordalis Junior G.S. Cuando mi hijo cumplió los dos años de edad, me salió un viaje que estaba en proceso y me dieron residencia. Tuve que dejar a mi hijo con su padre para venir a los Estados Unidos. Vine para buscar un mejor futuro para todos. He sufrido mucho porque tuve que dejar a mi hijo y a su padre. Estoy muy orgullosa del padre de mi hijo por que él ha soportado muy bien conmigo y con nuestro hijo. Por eso quiero trabajar duro para traerlo a conocer este país y para ayudar a mi familia.

Quiero que mi madre traiga a mi padre. Él es el mejor padre del mundo. Nosotros llegamos a los Estados Unidos con mi madre porque a nosotros nos pidió mi abuelo, el padre de mami. Tuvimos que dejar a papi y a mi hijo y esposo, pero cuando tengamos los recursos los traeremos si Dios quiere. El padre de mi hijo es un buen padre porque cuando el niño y yo más lo necesitamos él está con nosotros. Por ejemplo, cuando mi hijo estuvo internado por una semana y el niño estaba muy enfermo, su padre estaba con él todo el tiempo a su lado porque yo no estuve allá. Gracias a Dios el niño salió del peligro y ahora es un niño sano y muy inteligente.

Estoy trabajando para cuando pueda ir para mi país a ver a mi familia. Cuando tengo los recursos, voy a traerlos a los Estados Unidos. Tengo cuatros meses en los Estados Unidos y me gusta este país porque es un país desarrollado. Un consejo que yo daría a las jóvenes es que no se casen jovenes. Esperen hasta que su tiempo le llegue y piensen en las cosas antes de hacerlas.

Separation Causes a Family Harm

Cesar

Dominican Republic

I was born in San Pedro de Macoris in Miramar. It has been ten years since my mother came to the Bronx leaving us—her five children—in the Dominican Republic with our father. At that time, I was nine years old. We were a happy family, but when my parents separated, the problems began.

We practically lived by ourselves, because our father left with his woman. That hurt me because I felt a little lonely at times. We lived with our aunt and uncle, but it was never the same. They did not give us advice. My brothers, the two oldest in the family, worked in the area. They took care of us, and we always tried to do our best and cooked for ourselves. My oldest brother worried about taking care of us, especially our brother who is deaf-mute. I am the youngest of my brothers and I follow my eldest brother. Even though I am younger than my brother who is deaf-mute, I always looked after him. I raised him, not my mom. We communicate through sign language and we understand each other. We always used to play and we loved each other dearly.

But he was also the most foolish of us all. I was always fighting with him in the street so that he wouldn't do anything bad. I went looking for him in El Malecon; I took him out of the town, away from his friends. They were my friends too, but I didn't want him to be with them. People used him because he was deaf-mute. They introduced him to drugs. He didn't know what he was doing, and he didn't understand that he was doing something bad.

My brother and I were the only ones from our family who came together to live with my mother here in New York in my aunt's house. We were fine, but it wasn't the same as being in our own home. While she was gone, my mother had also lost her job. She didn't know what to do. A cousin of mine, who lived in Pennsylvania, called her and explained that there was work there. So I told her, "Mami, I'm going over there to see if I find a job. I will come back when we get more settled and I can study." I lasted three months in Pennsylvania. I didn't like it because you need to have a car and it is so rural. I realized it was not what I wanted and came back to the Bronx.

My mother's friend had connections with a shelter, a place for people who don't have a place to live. My brother and my mother moved to the shelter, but we had a lot of conflicts with my brother because there were people who wanted him to get involved with drugs. I also started working at a McDonald's to help them. We only spent three more months there, and then an apartment was found for us, and we could finally stay together in our own place. Luckily, my brother started changing his behavior. We have been through a lot, but I still love him dearly.

La Separación Ocasiona Daños En La Familia

Cesar
Dominican Republic

Nací en San Pedro de Macorís en Miramar. Hace 10 años atrás mi madre ingresó al Bronx dejándonos—sus cinco hijos—en la Republica Dominicana con nuestro padre. En esa época yo tenía nueve años de edad. Éramos una familia feliz pero cuando se separaron mis padres comenzaron los problemas.

Nosotros prácticamente vivíamos solos porque mi papá se fue con su mujer. Eso me afectó porque me sentía un poquito solo a veces. Vivimos con mi tía y tío pero nunca fue lo mismo. Ellos no nos daban consejos… Los hermanos míos, los dos más grandes trabajan en la zona. Entonces ellos nos cuidaban a nosotros y nosotros siempre tratábamos de ser lo mejor y cocinábamos para nosotros mismos. Mi hermano mayor se preocupa por cuidarnos a todos nosotros especialmente a mi hermano sordomudo. Yo soy el más pequeño de mis hermanos y le sigo a él. Aunque yo soy más pequeño que él, siempre estaba pendiente de él. Se crió conmigo y no con mi mamá. Nos comunicamos por seña y nos entendemos. Entonces, nosotros siempre vivíamos jugando y nos queríamos mucho.

Pero él es el más necio de todos. Siempre vivía peleando con él en la calle para que no haga nada malo. Lo iba buscar al malecón, lo sacaba de su parranda, de sus amiguitos. También eran amigos míos pero no me gustaba que estuviera con ellos. La gente lo usaban por ser sordomudo y lo metieron a la droga. El no sabía lo que estaba haciendo y pensaba que estaba haciendo lo bueno.

Cuando ingresé a este país, vinimos solamente él y yo aquí a Nueva York con mi madre en la casa de una tía mía. Estábamos bien pero no es lo mismo que estar en nuestra casa. Mi mamá también había perdido el trabajo. No sabía que hacer. Un primo mío que vivía en Pensilvania la llamó y le explicó que allá había trabajo. Entonces yo le dije, "Mami, yo voy para allá para ver si consigo un trabajo. Vuelvo cuando estamos más estables y yo puedo estudiar." Duré tres meses en Pensilvania. No me gustó porque hay que tener vehiculo y es como un campo. Entonces yo pensé que eso no era lo que yo quería y vine de nuevo para el Bronx.

Una amiga de mi mamá tenía relaciones con un shelter, un lugar para personas que no tienen donde ubicarse. Nos mudaron a un shelter, pero tuvimos muchos conflictos con mi hermano porque habían personas que lo querían usar y fumaba droga. Empecé a trabajar en un McDonalds para ayudarlos. Nada más duramos tres meses más y nos buscaron un apartamento y pude estar con mi hermano. Por suerte, empezó a cambiar su forma de ser. Pasamos por muchas cosas, pero lo quiero mucho.

How Would You Feel?

Santos Memories
Dominican Republic

My name is Santos, and I was born in Santo Domingo January 2nd, 1991. When I was five years old, I liked to play with dogs a lot, and I adored them. But there was one day that something crossed my mind. I considered what would happen if I put a stick in the mouth of my neighbor's dog. A moment arrived when the dog started barking at me a lot, and that's when I put the stick in its mouth. The dog got a hold of my hand and bit me. It was very painful and I went running to my grandmother, who put something on my hand for the bite. My grandmother told me, "For being foolish, bad things happen, and you are not going to play with dogs anymore to avoid something worse." After that, I played with dolls with my cousins, even though I didn't really like to. I played with them when I could to avoid boredom. But I liked toy cars more. When I was little girl, I liked everything that was for boys.

I came to this country when I was 15 years old. Since then, I have been here with my entire family. We have been living here for three years, and because of that, I feel more comfortable. For all the time that I have been here, I've lived with my father and my brothers. Upon arriving in New York, I liked it because I didn't end up living somewhere where I felt uncomfortable. But at first, I did, because I wasn't with my mother, and I felt lonely. I also didn't trust other people, but with time, I have grown to care a lot for my aunt and others. They gained my trust, because they took us out so that we'd get to know New York City well.

People's lives change greatly when they come over here. You get used to the customs and ways of living here, and people change for better or for worse. What I like about New York is its different communities. It's something that you can't find in other countries. For example, there are different cultures that one can get to know here, also languages and customs. I really like Muslim culture and their dances. I have danced it on some occasions. The language that grabs my attention the most is Italian and also English, of course. They are pretty much the ones I am interested in for now.

Now I am going to talk about something that was very important in my life. Andres Santos was the name of my grandfather, whom we loved so dearly, and he died on June 18th, 2009. He was only 86 years old. He still had life in him to share with those he loved most—his family members, who loved him so much. He took care of all of his grandchildren and his children, as well as others, even if they weren't his own.

When my father found out, my aunts didn't know what to do. We were in charge of buying the tickets for the flights and organizing the luggage, finding the passports, and buying anything else that they needed. We were worried, waiting for at least a phone call to figure out how to remain strong. It was twelve at night when they called to tell us that things were very serious. We began crying because we knew the reality of the situation.

When my uncle finally called, it was at seven in the morning, to tell us that our grandfather had died due to asphyxia. I thought that the earth had been shaken by a single blow. What hurt the most was that we couldn't go, because we had to watch the house and our brothers, and most of all to go to school. But the anger didn't let me think, analyze, or sort my thoughts knowing that I had lost the most beautiful thing in my life. I loved him so much, because I was raised with him, and we shared a lot of things when he would get sick. He took care of me a lot and I took care of him a lot.

When you feel like the air escapes from you and you can't breathe, and you think that everything in the world has left with that person, I remind you that it is normal, because our hearts aren't made from stone. I miss you, Papá. You are the light of inspiration in my life, the most prized treasure of all. Light wouldn't exist if you weren't in heaven amongst the stars. Thank you for everything.

¿Cómo Te Sentirías Perder a Alguien Tan Especial en Tu Vida?

Santos Memories
Dominican Republic

Nací en Santo Domingo en 1991 día 2 de enero. Cuando yo tenia 5 años, a mí me gustaba jugar mucho con los perros y lo adoraba mucho. Pero hubo un día que me pasó algo por la mente. Pensé en que pasara si le entraba un palo en la boca del perro de mi vecino. Entonces llegó ese momento y el perro comenzó a ladrarme mucho y ahí fue cuando le entre el palo en la boca. El perro llego a agarrarme la mano y me mordió. Eso me dolió mucho y yo me fui corriendo para donde mi abuela que me untó algo para la mordida. Mi abuela me dijo, "Por tú estar de necia, todo te pasa y ya no vuelvas a jugar con perros para que después no te pase algo peor." Después de eso, me puse a jugar con las muñecas con mis primas aunque no me gustaba mucho hacerlo. Yo trataba de jugar con ellas para no aburrirme. Pero lo que más me gusta son los carritos. Cuando era una niña, todo lo que era de niño me gustaban.

Yo vine a este país cuando tenía 15 años. Todo ese tiempo tengo aquí con todas mi familia. Ya tenemos 3 años viviendo aquí y por eso estoy más cómoda. Por todo el tiempo que tengo aquí estoy con mi padre y mis hermanos. Al llegar a Nueva York, a mí me gustó porque yo no llegué a una parte que me sentía indiferente. Pero a lo primero sí porque no estaba con mi mamá y me sentía sola. También no le tenía confianza a los de más pero después, con el tiempo, le tomé mucho cariño a mi tía y a los de más. Se ganaron mi cariño porque nos sacaban a pasear para que conociéramos bien la ciudad de Nueva York.

La vida de las personas cuando llegan aquí cambia mucho. Pero después te acostumbras a las costumbres y maneras porque en todo este tiempo, las personas cambian para mejor o para peor. Lo que me gusta de Nueva York es las comunidades que tiene. Una manera que no hay en otros países. Por ejemplo, como las diferentes culturas que uno puede conocer aquí. Y también el lenguaje y costumbres que hay aquí. Me encanta mucho la cultura musulman y sus bailes. Lo he bailado en algunas ocasiones. El lenguaje que más me llama a la atención es el italiano y el inglés por supuesto. Yo sé que esos son, más o menos los que me gustan a mí por ahora.

Ahora le voy hablar de algo que fue muy importante en mi vida. Andrés Santos se llamaba mi abuelo que tanto queríamos y murió el día 18 de junio del 2009. A penas tenía 86 años. El tenía toda la vida por delante para compartir con los seres que más quería como sus familiares que tanto lo queríamos. El cuidaba a todos sus nietos y sus hijos y lo de más aunque no lo fueran.

Cuando mi papá se entero, mis tías y lo de más no sabían que hacer. Nosotros nos encargamos de comprar los vuelos y organizarle su equipaje, buscarle sus pasaportes, y comprar lo que le hacía falta para llevar. Nosotros nos quedamos preocupados esperando aunque sea una llamada para saber como seguía de salud. Eran las 12 de la noche cuando nos llamaron para decirnos que estaba muy grave. Nosotros comenzamos a llorar porque sabíamos la realidad de las cosas.

Cuando al fin mi tío llamó, eran las 7 de las mañana para decirnos que nuestro abuelo había muerto de un asfixie. Yo pensaba que el mundo se había de rumbado de un solo golpe. Lo que más nos dolió fue que no podíamos ir porque teníamos que cuidar la casa y nuestros hermanos y principalmente, ir a la escuela. Pero el coraje no me dejaba pensar ni analizar ni aclárala mis ideas de saber que perdí lo más bello de mi vida. Yo lo quería mucho porque yo me crié con él y compartíamos muchas cosas cuando él se enfermaba. El me cuidaba mucho y yo a él también.

Cuando tú sientes que el aire se te va y no puedes respirar, que piensas que todo en el mundo se te fue con esa persona, le repito que es normal porque nuestros corazones no son de hierro. Te extraño papá. Tú eres la luz de la inspiración en mi vida, mi tesoro más apreciado para todos. La luz no existiera si no estuvieras en el cielo junto a las estrellas. Gracias por todo.

Soccer is Just Like a War, but Sometimes Much More Than a War

Moussa Sinerna

The Gambia

My name is Moussa Sinerna. I'm from Gambia, West Africa. I was born on April 10th, 1991. I grew up in the village called Carawol. When I was young, I was a very good soccer player. I passed the tryouts, and I qualified to play for the school team. At that time I was only seven years old; I was the youngest player on the team. When we went to our first game of the middle schools tournament, my coach sat me out. He said I was too young to play in the game. I was sad about that. I was so upset that I couldn't even watch my teammates play, and we lost the game, one to zero.

In the second game, the coach said, "Moussa, you can try this game." He put me in with the starting eleven. I started playing as a forward. I did well, but I couldn't score. The first half finished with the score zero to zero. When we came back to the second half, I tried a long shot from the corner with seven minutes to go. I scored a goal, and we won, one to zero. We went to the semi-finals, too. The coach promised me that if I tried like I had in my other game, he would give me a surprise gift. I sat down and I asked myself, "What am I supposed to do to prepare?" "I think," I said, "I am supposed to train hard, like five hours a day, so that I can get 100% fit." I kept on training, and then we went to the finals, and we won the trophy and the final game, three to two. I was the leading goal scorer in the tournament, and they gave me the medal "Young Best Player." That's like MVP in the USA. I felt very proud, and my coach gave me gifts—money and new soccer cleats. After the tournament, I became famous in my school.

After the tournament, my school team's coach, Mr. Balajo, started to choose his 18-boy squad for the next school tournament. I was in the squad that he chose. We started training with our coach before the games. All the players had new cleats. I remember I had Nike soccer shoes that were my first pair of Nike shoes ever. The first game of the tournament was on June 10th, 1998. The school bus took us and our fans to the playing ground. We went to the dressing room with Coach Balajo. He selected his starting eleven, and I was in the starting line-up.

The referee blew the whistle. The game started immediately. The ball kept moving around, up and down the field. The coach called over the captain of the team and told him to tell his teammates to calm down. Quickly, we did as he said. With 37 minutes left in the game, there was a long ball from the center. I did a strong run, struggling to catch up to the ball. I dribbled the ball between two defenders. I saw my teammate moving into a very good position; I crossed the ball for him, he chested it and scored the first goal in the game. We started celebrating that goal! I turned around and saw our fans cheering like a group of birds.

The referee blew the whistle for halftime. We went to the dressing room. The coach said "Good job!" to the team. We went back for the second half. The referee blew the whistle. We got back the ball. I was the forward, as a second striker, and got tackled near the goal box. It was so painful; I thought my leg was broken, but soon it felt better. I heard the whistle for the foul committed on me; it sounded like screaming. It was my free kick. I took the ball and put it on the ground. The referee counted ten yards from the wall. I used my right foot to kick the ball. I made sure the ball passed the wall. The ball curved around all the players. Very soon, I saw the ball in the net and started to run, celebrating the second goal! All my teammates were jumping and celebrating with me. I turned around and I saw my coach celebrating. The goal was scored in the stoppage time of the game and the referee blew the last whistle of the game. It was over, two to zero. I turned around, and I saw all the fans cheering.

As soon as the game was over, I exchanged my shirt with the guy who had been marking me. I shook his hand and said, "Thanks, good game," but he was a little nervous about the loss, because they needed the game, like we needed it, but they hadn't won. It was a joy for us, but life is like that; sometimes you will be the happiest person, and sometimes you will be the saddest person. Soccer is like a war, because if your team is playing against the top team, it looks like a war. No one wants to lose.

My coach called all of the players to the dressing room and he said, "Congratulations, my boys! Well done! Good job!" and he clapped. When we returned to school on Monday, there was an assembly. The head teacher began his speech with, "Thank you, my boys. You did what I wanted you to do, and I like that very much. I have something for you guys after the assembly." Later, we went to his office and he gave us each a certificate.

When I was 15 years old, we went to the capital city called Banjul, and I joined a junior school over there. I was on a soccer team there, too. When I was new to that team, I went to the field every day to practice with them. They didn't know me, and I didn't know a lot of people. I would always go the corner and sit by myself, watching them. And then, little by little, I worked with them, and I got to know everybody. Then, I started playing with them, and they learned to respect and honor me. They saw what I could do, and I saw what they could do. I won lots of cups for them; I won three trophies. At that time I was 16 and 17, and then, I came to America.

When I was about 15 years old, my mom went to America. I was left with my three brothers. She got a green card, and then she filed for my brothers and me, and we came to America. At that time, I was 17 years old. My first week in the USA, I started going to Bronx Regional High School. I started studying for my high school degree, and I'm still working on it. I would really like to play soccer, but when I came to America, I couldn't find a soccer team. That's why I'm a little bit nervous. I really miss being on a soccer team. Even my parents wanted me to be a soccer player in the USA. They bought new soccer cleats for me. I went to the park with new friends in the Bronx. They are different people—a different color than me and race too, but I always play soccer with them. I have a dream that one day I will participate for the United States and I will work hard to win many trophies for the country. God bless the Americans; they trust in God.

My message is that when you are young, you have to try to get your education. When you are young, you have to do something to make sure that tomorrow you can take care of your family, too, so that you can live a better life.

My Heart

Ramon Noel Tavarez
Dominican Republic

I have been here for two years and four months, but I was born in the Dominican Republic. When I came to the United States, I was 16 years old. In Santo Domingo, I was fine, because I was studying a lot and I liked the social science readings. That class inspired me, and I got good grades in it. Then, with time, I was in a higher grade, but my mom decided to bring me here.

At first, I didn't like it. I found it strange, because when I was in Santo Domingo, they painted another picture for me. They told me, "It is like this… it is like that." It sounded like heaven, but when I got here, it was far from it. When I came, I said to myself, "This is not my country, I think it's ugly." So, I did not find it to be the same as life in Santo Domingo, but one learns to adapt to everything. So I began adapting to this country.

Here in the Bronx, my mom was confused about the school enrollment, and she put me in the eighth grade. But I was much too old to be in such a low grade. So, because of that, I am not more advanced. In the eighth grade, they used to give me a lot of readings about a tale of a guy named Panchito, who came to the United States from Mexico. Panchito's life was not easy because he did not know English. His friends who knew English and Spanish ridiculed him, until one day, he decided to learn English. He set his mind on English and dedicated himself to his studies until he finally learned English. Then, everything that his friends talked about, he understood. He never said anything, but he went and spoke to his teachers and told them that the other students were making fun of him. But then, since he had learned English, they wanted to be friends, and since he didn't hold any grudges, he became friends with them. They became great company and Panchito gave them advice—to not ridicule others, because that was bad. The group felt bad that he had gone through that. And so that's what happened, they united and became great friends. I can remember this story because it inspired me a lot. That story made me put myself in Panchito's shoes for that moment and I realized that I could act as Panchito. I embraced the story. It really made me focus, because his was the same life I was living.

My mom decided to sign me up here, in the GED program, because they said there were no problems here and that it was safer. I like the GED Plus program because I am learning at a rapid pace, and I pay more attention to classes. I also think that I am learning because I converse with my brother. I have two brothers, one is 20 and the other is 23 years old, who take English courses at Fordham. I see that my brothers are becoming more intelligent. I'm noticing that they use more English words, and I hear them speaking more eloquently. In the future, my goal is to become an engineer, a consulting engineer. That's why mathematics inspires me. Every class inspires me, but the one that I care to be smarter in is mathematics.

I have a wife in Santo Domingo. Her name is Fabiola, and she is five months pregnant. One of my goals is to bring her here, to the United States. She is 17 years old, with a light-skinned Native American complexion. She is about five feet seven inches tall. She has brown eyes and red hair. I thank her because she loves me a lot, and I love her, too. I go see her whenever I can, but for now, I am thinking about going in the summer to see my baby be born. My baby will be named Noel Tavarez, after my middle name.

I feel happy because I am going to be a father, and this is going to be my first child. I am already anxious about becoming a father. I hope that God lets me see my baby when he is going to be born. I can't wait to teach him many important things about life like respecting others, being well educated, and much more. I want to bring my wife and child here, so that they can start a new life, and I know that it'll be better because there are many opportunities.

Everything that I have written in this book I hold deep inside my heart. Thank you for everything that you are teaching me Ms. Rodriguez, Ms. Wood, Ms. Arcos, and Ms. Brown.

Mi Corazón

Ramon Noel Tavarez
Dominican Republic

Yo tengo 2 años y cuatro meses aquí pero nací en Republica Dominicana. Cuando llegué a los Estados Unidos tenía 16 años de edad. En Santo Domingo me fue bien porque yo estaba estudiando mucho y me gustaba la lectura de ciencias sociales. Esa clase me inspiraba y sacaba buenas notas en ella. Después con el tiempo, yo estaba en un alto grado, pero mi mamá decidió traerme para acá.

A lo primero, no me gustó. Lo veía extraño porque cuando yo estaba en Santo Domingo me pintaban otra cosa. Me decían, "Esto es así… esto es así." Me lo imaginaba como un paraíso, pero cuando llegué, no fue así. Cuando yo llegue yo decía, "Esto no es mi país, yo lo hallo feo." Entonces, no me lo hallaba igual, pero uno a todo se adapta. Entonces me fui adaptando a este país.

Aquí en el Bronx, mi mamá se equivoco y me puso en el octavo grado. Pero yo era muy mayor para estar en ese grado tan bajito. Entonces por eso, yo no estoy más avanzado. En el octavo grado, me daban mucha lectura sobre un cuento de un muchacho que se llamaba Panchito, que vino de México a los Estados Unidos. La vida de Panchito no era fácil porque él no sabía inglés. Los amigos que sabían inglés y español se burlaban de él hasta que el decidió aprender inglés. Puso la mente para inglés y nada más se dedicaba para su estudio hasta que aprendió inglés. Después, todo lo que hablaban los amigos, él lo entendía. Y él entonces se quedaba callado e iba y hablaba con los maestros y le decía que los otros estudiantes se estaban burlando de él. Y después como él aprendió inglés, ellos se querían unir con él y como él no guardaba rencor, el se unió con ellos. Se hicieron buena compañía y después Panchito le daba consejos a sus amigos de que no se burlaran de los otros porque eso era malo. El grupo se sentía mal como el ya había pasado por eso. Entonces eso fue lo que se sucedió hasta que se unieron e hicieron buena compañía. Yo puedo recordar bien esta historia porque me inspiró mucho. Me hizo ponerme en el lugar de Panchito por ese momento y yo vi que podía actuar como Panchito. Yo saboreé la historia. Esa me hizo enfocar mucho porque era la misma vida que yo estaba viviendo.

Mi mamá me decidió apuntarme aquí en el programa de GED porque decían que aquí no había problema, que era más seguro, y aquí me siento bien. El programa de GED PLUS me gusta porque estoy aprendiendo rápido y presto más atención a las clases. También yo sospecho que estoy aprendiendo porque dialogo con mi hermano. Tengo dos hermanos, uno de 20 y otro de 23 años, que cogen cursos de inglés en Fordham. Estoy viendo que mis hermanos se están poniendo más inteligentes. Estoy escuchando que dicen más palabras en inglés y oigo que mis hermanos hablan de una manera más educada. En el futuro, mi meta es ser ingeniero, ingeniero consultor. Por eso me inspira mucho la matemática. Todas las clases me inspiran pero la que me preocupa para ser más inteligente es la matemática.

Tengo mi esposa en Santo Domingo. El nombre de mi esposa es Fabiola y ella tiene 5 meses de embarazo. Vive en mi casa en Santo Domingo con mi tía y mi tío. Una de mis metas es traer a mi esposa aquí, a los Estado Unidos. Tiene 17 años de edad, color india clarita. Mide más o menos como 5 pies y 7 pulgadas de altura. Tiene ojos marrones y el pelo rojo. La agradezco porque ella me quiere mucho y yo también la quiero. Yo voy a verla cuando puedo. Pero por ahora, estoy pensando ir en el verano a ver mi baby cuando valla a nacer. Mi baby se llamará Noel Tavarez, como mi segundo nombre.

Yo me siento feliz porque voy a ser papá y este será mi primer baby. Ya tengo ansiedad de ser papá. Yo espero en Dios que me deje ver mi bebé nacer cuando vaya a nacer. Y ya quiero enseñarle muchas cosas importantes de la vida como respetar a los de más, ser bien educado y muchas cosas más. Quiero traer mi esposa y mi baby cuando nazca para que tengan una nueva vida y sé que aquí será mejor porque hay mucha capacidad.

Todo lo que he dicho en este libro lo llevo muy dentro de mi corazón. Gracias por todo lo que me están enseñando mis maestras: Ms. Rodriguez, Ms. Wood, Ms. Arcos, y Ms. Brown.

My Baby

Lilibeth Vargas
Dominican Republic

When I found out I was pregnant, I didn't tell anybody, because I was scared about what my mom and my boyfriend would say. Then, when I was one month pregnant, I told my boyfriend. He wanted the baby, too, so he told me, "Oh, just tell your mother that you're pregnant." I was like, "No, I don't want to tell my mom."

When my mom found out, I was five months pregnant. I waited because I was scared. She had asked me and I said, "No, I'm not pregnant." Then, I went to the Dominican Republic for one month, and when I came back, I told my older sister, and she told my mom. My mom was crying because she was happy! She asked me, "Oh, why didn't you tell me?" I went to the hospital with her to do the sonogram, and she cried when they did it. My boyfriend cried, too!

When I was in the hospital, oh my goodness…that was a lot of pain. My labor was from eight-thirty am to four-thirty am on July 3rd, 2009. Twenty hours! I was telling my mom, "Oh, I want to go home, I want to go home!" And she was telling me, "No, no, you can't, you have to give birth." I was like, "No, no, no, I want to go home, I want to go home!" I was crying because there was a lot of pain, a lot of pain. Then when my baby was born, I cried from happiness, and my boyfriend and my sister and my mother were all there. I was crying because I saw my baby for the first time. She looked so beautiful, like an angel. When I was in the hospital, I didn't sleep the whole night because I was looking at my baby.

When my baby was two months, she got a fever and I went to the Emergency Room. I went at six o'clock pm, and I came back home at three am. Two days later they called me, "Oh, you have to come back. We have to take blood." They told me, "Oh, your baby might have an infection in her blood." We stayed in the hospital for three days, and I couldn't sleep because she was up all night crying.

And I was lonely, 'cause they told me "Oh, your mom can't stay, nobody can stay, only you." They told me, "Oh, they can come but they have to leave at nine o'clock." And one time, my boyfriend, he was telling me, "Oh, I want to stay." Then, when the nurse came, like at twelve, he had to leave. During the day when my mom was there, I slept. My baby got antibiotics, for like two months, or three.

I was so proud, too, when my baby talked for the first time. The first time she said "Papá," she was five and a half months old. When she said "Mamá" it was December 24th. She always says, "qué, qué, qué, qué." That's a word in Spanish that means "what" in English. The nurse told me she's very young to say words.